Publications of the

MINNESOTA HISTORICAL SOCIETY

RUSSELL W. FRIDLEY
Director

JEAN A. BROOKINS
Assistant Director
For Research and Publications

A Supplement to Reference Guide to Minnesota History

A Subject Bibliography, 1970-80

Compiled by Michael Brook
and Sarah P. Rubinstein

MINNESOTA HISTORICAL SOCIETY PRESS • ST. PAUL • 1983

Library of Congress Cataloging in Publication Data

Brook, Michael.
A supplement to Reference guide to Minnesota history,
1970-80.
(Publications of the Minnesota Historical Society)
Includes index.
1. Minnesota—Bibliography. I. Rubinstein, Sarah P.
(Sarah Paskins), 1942-   II. Brook, Michael.
Reference guide to Minnesota history. III. Title.
Z1299.B76 Suppl. [F606]   016.9776   83-5438
ISBN 0-87351-160-3 (pbk.)

Table of Contents

Introduction

THIS BIBLIOGRAPHY is a supplement to the *Reference Guide to Minnesota History: A Subject Bibliography of Books, Pamphlets, and Articles in English*, compiled by Michael Brook and published in 1974 by the Minnesota Historical Society. A project to prepare this supplement began in 1979 when it became evident that students, scholars, librarians, and others interested in the state's history would benefit from a guide to the substantial amount of Minnesota historical material issued between 1970 and 1980. Included in the 1,600 entries are some pre–1970 works and a handful of post–1980 publications, as well as reprint editions of several titles that appeared in the first bibliography. For a more complete explanation of the criteria used for selecting and classifying the entries, readers should be sure to refer to the introduction to the 1974 bibliography.

Some interesting publishing trends became apparent to the compilers of this bibliography. Not surprisingly, the celebration of the nation's bicentennial motivated Minnesotans to examine and write about their history. During the past decade many towns and churches in the state reached either a 75th or a 100th anniversary and commemorated the occasion with a published history. As a result, by far the largest category in this guide is "Local History," closely followed by "Religion." For similar reasons, population and immigration also became engrossing topics in 1970–80. Conversely, the fur trade, discovery and exploration, pioneer life, the Civil War, and travel accounts lost much of their appeal. Minnesota's Indian people are still the subject of a great many books and articles, although the historians' focus has shifted somewhat.

The major source of information on local government and community clubs and organizations remains the published town and county histories. County, city, and township governments and fraternal, mutual benefit, and social organizations and clubs generally have not drawn much attention from researchers. Agribusiness and social questions also are open fields for study.

The same basic arrangement used in the first bibliography has been retained in this guide, with a few exceptions. Each entry is placed under the subject heading most nearly applicable and appears only once. Readers researching a particular topic are therefore reminded to consult the index for all items pertaining to the subject. Some headings have been changed to reflect the contents and the number of works included under them. In the major category "General Surveys and Reference Works," for example, some shifts in the placement of subtopics can be noted. Three major categories were eliminated. "Minnesota Boundaries" appears with "Maps" as a subheading under "Geography"; "Minnesota and the Civil War" and "Minnesota and Foreign Wars" were combined as "Minnesotans in Military Service"; and "Printing and Publishing" became the subheading, "Books, Newspapers, and Journalists," in the "Communications" category.

Because fewer works on exploration, the fur trade, and pioneer life were published in 1970–80, several subheadings in those categories no longer exist. Other subjects were dropped from the categories of "Indians," "Government of Minnesota," "Politics and Parties," "The Arts," "Business, Industry, and Trade," "Health and Medicine," "Agriculture," and "Social Questions."

In the "Population and Immigration" category, two subheadings were created for the Finns and Mexican Americans, while the Irish and slavery and abolition disappeared as distinct subjects. Several publications in the growing field of "Communications" gave rise to a new subheading on "Radio, Television, and Telephone."

Only a few style changes appear in this supplement. Minnesota's Indian people are referred to as Dakota and Ojibway, the Uprising of 1862 is now the Dakota War, and Afro–Americans are called Blacks.

The books, pamphlets, and articles listed in this bibliography are in the English language only. No manuscripts, graduate theses, or newspaper articles have been included. Several fine guides to these kinds of materials already exist and are listed in the introduction to the 1974 bibliography.

In a time when many special interest histories are being issued in a photographic form, it became a challenge to determine just what was a published work. If internal evidence indicated that a history had been widely circulated—that is, to an entire town, church congregation, or business firm—then the work was included. The compilers made every effort to assure that listed items would be readily available either at the Minnesota Historical Society's Reference Library or at major libraries throughout the state. They reviewed each published work before the title was included.

For each entry the author, if there is one, appears first. The title comes next, followed by the publishing information. If the place of publication is known, it is listed, unless it forms part of the publisher's name. All places are within Minnesota unless stated otherwise or the place is well known. The publisher is omitted if it is the same as the author or issuer of the publication. If information comes from a source other than the work itself, it is placed in brackets, and if its accuracy is in doubt, a question mark is added. The number of pages appears in brackets if the work is not paginated. If a work is multi-volume, the number of volumes is substituted for pages. If a work has a bibliography or biographical sketches, that information is included. The abbreviations used are standard; MHS is used for Minnesota Historical Society and *MH* for *Minnesota History*.

The compilers of this bibliography wish to acknowledge the assistance given them by several individuals—Patrick K. Coleman, Patricia C. Harpole, and other staff members of the MHS Reference Library; Bruce M. White, Alan R. Woolworth, and Deborah L. Miller of the MHS Publications and Research Division. Michael Brook gathered the initial data for this project while he was on leave from the library of the University of Nottingham, England. Sarah P. Rubinstein continued the project and classified and edited the entries.

A Supplement to Reference Guide to Minnesota History, 1970-80

GENERAL SURVEYS AND REFERENCE WORKS

Andreas, A. T. *An Illustrated Historical Atlas of the State of Minnesota*. Chicago: The Author, 1874. Reprinted, Evansville, Ind.: Unigraphic, Inc., 1976.

Blegen, Theodore C. *Minnesota: A History of the State*. Minneapolis: Univ. of Minn. Press, 1963. 688 p. With bibliog. Reprinted 1975 with additional chapter, "A State That Works," by Russell W. Fridley. Added readings.

Borchert, John R. and Donald P. Yaeger. *Atlas of Minnesota Resources and Settlement*. Rev. ed. St. Paul: Minn. State Planning Agency, 1969. 261 p. 1st ed. published 1968. With bibliog.

Carpenter, Allan. *Minnesota*. (New Enchantment of America Series.) Rev. ed. Chicago: Childrens Press, 1978. First published 1966. 96 p.

Currents. Vol. 1–. Shakopee, 1978–. Published quarterly by Minnesota Valley Restoration Project, Inc.

Lass, William E. *Minnesota: A Bicentennial History*. (States and the Nation Series.) New York: Norton, 1977. 224 p. With bibliog.

Minnesota Genealogist. Vol. 1–. St. Paul, 1970–. Published quarterly by the Minn. Genealogical Soc. Vols. 1–10 (1970–79) indexed. St. Paul: The Society, 1979.

Minnesota Historical Society. *Gopher Historian*. Vols. 1–26. St. Paul, 1946–72. Junior magazine of history published three times each year. Annual indexes published beginning with vol. 6. *A Complete Index to the Gopher Historian, 1946–1972*. St. Paul: MHS, 1977.

Neill, Edward D. *The History of Minnesota: From the Earliest French Explorations to the Present Time*. 5th ed. Minneapolis: Minn. Historical Co., 1883. 929 p. Earlier eds.: Philadelphia: Lippincott, 1858, 1872; Minneapolis: Johnson, Smith & Harrison, 1878; Minneapolis: Minn. Historical Co., 1882. Reprint of 1858 ed., New York: Arno Press, 1975.

Ostendorf, Paul J. *Every Person's Name Index to An Illustrated Historical Atlas of the State of Minnesota*. Winona: St. Mary's College, 1979. 100 p. Index to A. T. Andreas, *Atlas*.

Parker, Nathan H. *The Minnesota Handbook for 1856-7*. Boston: John P. Jewett, 1857. 159 p. Reprinted, New York: Arno Press, 1975.

Poatgieter, A. Hermina and James T. Dunn, eds. *Gopher Reader: Minnesota's Story in Words and Pictures— Selections from the* Gopher Historian. 2 vols. St. Paul: MHS, 1958, 1975. Vol. 1 published jointly with Minn. Statehood Centennial Commission. Primarily for children.

Rowan, Thomas J., ed. *The Minnesota Almanac, 1977*. Minneapolis: Robert A. Jones, Publisher, 1976. 320 p. Information on crime, sports, disease, weather, state government, and agriculture.

Seitz, Peter. *A Minnesota Mosaic: The Bicentennial in Photographs*. Minneapolis: Minn. Am. Revolution Bicentennial Commission, 1977. 72 p.

Vexler, Robert I., ed. *Chronology and Documentary Handbook of the State of Minnesota*. Dobbs Ferry, N.Y.: Oceana Publications, 1978. 146 p. With biographies.

Whitson, Skip, comp. *Minnesota and Manitoba 100 years ago*. Albuquerque, N.M.: Sun Pub. Co., 1977. Minn., pp. 4–22. Reprinted from *Harper's*, 1875.

Works Projects Administration, Minnesota. *Works Progress Administration Accomplishments: Minnesota, 1935-1939*. [St. Paul?, 1939?]. 214 p. A photographic history.

Archives and Manuscripts Collections

Fogerty, James E., comp. *Manuscripts Collections of the Minnesota Regional Research Centers: Guide Number 2*. St. Paul: MHS, 1979. 92 p.

———. *Preliminary Guide to the Holdings of the Minnesota Regional Research Centers*. St. Paul: MHS, 1975. 20 p. Lists manuscripts and oral history interviews.

Fridley, Russell W. "Interpretive Centers: An Indigenous Minnesota Idea That Is Thriving!" in *MH*, 45:32–34 (Spring, 1976).

———. "Should Public Papers Be Private Property?" in *MH*, 44:37–39 (Spring, 1974).

Hinding, Andrea and others, eds. *Women's History Sources: A Guide to Archives and Manuscript Collections in the United States.* New York: R. R. Bowker Co., 1979. 2 vols. Minn., 1:512–589.

Lucas, Lydia A., comp. *Manuscripts Collections of the Minnesota Historical Society: Guide Number 3.* St. Paul: MHS, 1977. 189 p.

———. "Yorktown Campaign Is Featured in Allyn K. Ford Collection," in *MH*, 44:224–226 (Summer, 1975).

Martin, Virginia L. "The People's Choice: Reflections of the Political Process in MHS Collections," in *MH*, 45:70–74 (Summer, 1976).

Matters, Marion E., comp. *Minnesota State Archives: Preliminary Checklist.* St. Paul: MHS, 1979. 94 p.

Meissner, Dennis E. *Guide to the Use of the 1860 Minnesota Population Census Schedules and Index.* St. Paul: MHS, 1978. 21 p.

Northwest Minnesota Historical Center. *Guide to the Holdings: Northwest Minnesota Historical Center: A Regional Repository of the Minnesota Historical Society.* Comp. by David B. Olson. Moorhead: Moorhead State Univ., 1978. 42 p.

Storch, Neil T. *Guide to the Archives and Manuscripts of the Diocese of Duluth.* (Social Science Research Publications Series.) Duluth: Univ. of Minn., 1977. 16 p.

Swanson, Duane P. "Great Northern Records Readied for Researchers," in *MH*, 44:185–188 (Spring, 1975).

Bibliographies, Pictures, and Other Sources

Levenson, Rosaline. *Company Towns of the Minnesota Iron Ranges: A Bibliography of Historical and Current Sources.* (Public Administration Series: Bibliography P–412.) Monticello, Ill.: Vance Bibliographies, 1980. 25 p.

"Main Street," in *MH*, 43:222–227 (Summer, 1973). Mostly photographs, 1868–1925.

"[Minnesota Historical] Society Collects Animal Traps," in *MH*, 43:146–148 (Winter, 1972).

Minnesota Historical Society. *Historic Resources in Minnesota: A Report on Their Extent, Location, and Need for Preservation, Submitted to the Minnesota Legislature.* St. Paul, 1979. 172 p.

"Minnesota Trade Cards," in *MH*, 43:270–274 (Fall, 1973). Mostly photographs.

Mittlefehldt, Pamela J. *Minnesota Folklife: An Annotated Bibliography.* St. Paul: Center for the Study of Minn. Folklife and the MHS, 1979. 42 p.

Palmquist, Bonnie B. "Women in *Minnesota History*, 1915–1976: An Annotated Bibliography of Articles Pertaining to Women," in *MH*, 45:187–191 (Spring, 1977).

Pope, Wiley R. and Alissa L. Wiener. *Tracing Your Ancestors in Minnesota: A Guide to the Sources.* Rev. 2nd ed. St. Paul: Minn. Family Trees, 1980. 228 p. 1st ed. published 1978.

Swenson, Grace S. *Minnesota in Books for Young Readers: An Annotated Bibliography.* Burnsville: Voyageur Press, 1975. 150 p.

Treude, Mai. *Windows to the Past: A Bibliography of Minnesota County Atlases.* Minneapolis: Center for Urban and Regional Affairs, Univ. of Minn., 1980. 187 p.

Walrath, Ronald. "MHS Collections: [Newspapers]," in *MH*, 43:113–116 (Fall, 1972). Reprinted in shortened form as "The Media Collection of the Minnesota State Historical Society," in *Journalism History*, 1:26 (Spring, 1974).

Westbrook, Nicholas. "Decisions, Decisions: An Exhibit's Invisible Ingredient," in *MH*, 45:292–296 (Fall, 1977). MHS clothing collection.

U.S. Library of Congress. *United States Local Histories in the Library of Congress: A Bibliography.* Ed. by Marion J. Kaminkow. 5 vols. Baltimore: Magna Carta Book Co., 1975. "The Northwest," 4:139–157, 5:269; "Minnesota," 4:163–215, 5:271–274.

Collected Biographies

Haeg, Larry, Jr. *Heritage Northwest.* Minneapolis–St. Paul: WCCO Radio, 1976. 267 p. Contains many brief biographical sketches of Minnesotans.

Minnesota Territorial Pioneers. *Pioneer Chronicles.* Minneapolis, 1976. 319 p. Over 100 biographical sketches.

Stuhler, Barbara and Gretchen Kreuter, eds. *Women of Minnesota: Selected Biographical Essays.* St. Paul: MHS, 1977. 402 p. Contains 15 chapters on individuals (listed separately in this bibliography under their chief subject fields) together with "Brief Biographies of Other Minnesota Women," by Patricia C. Harpole, pp. 325–343.

Essays and Interpretations

Peirce, Neal R. *The Great Plains States of America: People, Politics, and Power in the Nine Great Plains States.* New York: Norton, 1972. "Minnesota: The Successful Society," pp. 110–150.

Perpich, Rudy. "Minnesota History and Heritage: Understanding Our Present by Understanding Our Past," in *MH*, 45:245–249 (Summer, 1977).

Russell, Arthur J. *One of Our First Families, and a Few Other Minnesota Essays.* Minneapolis: Leonard H. Wells, 1925. 119 p. Includes Philander Prescott family.

Youngdale, James M. "The Frontier: Economic Boom and Intellectual Bust," in *American Studies in Scandinavia* (Oslo, Nor.), 8:1–16 (1976). The American frontier as a symbol.

Historical Societies and Historians

"Bertha L. Heilbron, 1895–1972," in *MH*, 43:149–151 (Winter, 1972).

Cutright, Paul R. *A History of the Lewis and Clark Journals.* Norman: Univ. of Oklahoma Press, 1976. "Ernest Staples Osgood," pp. 145–176; C. A. Peairs, Jr., "Legal Aspects of *Minnesota Historical Society v. United States of America in re Lewis and Clark Expedition Papers*," pp. 265–269.

Flanagan, John T. *Theodore C. Blegen: A Memoir.* Northfield: Norwegian–Am. Historical Assn., 1977. 181 p. With bibliog. of Blegen's books.

Fridley, Russell W. "Critical Choices for the Minnesota Historical Society," in *MH*, 46:130–146 (Winter, 1978).

——. "A History of Minnesota Histories," in *MH*, 46:201–204 (Spring, 1979).

Kozlak, Mark J. *The Preservation of Historic Legacies in Hennepin County: An Analysis of the Programs of the Local Historical Societies.* [Minneapolis?]: Hennepin County Board of Commissioners, 1975. 54 p.

Lovoll, Odd S. and Kenneth O. Bjork. *The Norwegian–American Historical Association, 1925–1975.* Northfield: Norwegian–Am. Historical Assn., 1975. 72 p.

Historic Sites and Markers

Aguar, Charles E. *Exploring St. Louis County's Historical Sites.* Duluth: St. Louis County Historical Soc., 1971. 52 p. Update of 1st ed., published in 1966.

Aguar, Jyring, Whiteman, Moser [Co.] *Historic Sites and Treasures: An Initial Inventory of Mille Lacs County, Minnesota: Preliminary Report. Prepared for the Mille Lacs County Planning Advisory Commission.* Duluth, 1972. 40 p. With bibliog.

Architects IV, Fugelso, Porter, Simich, Whitman. *Restoration Plan for Old Calumet, Minnesota.* Duluth: Privately published, 1974. 44 p.

Architectural Resources, Inc. *A Master Plan for Split Rock Lighthouse Historic Site.* Duluth, 1977. 16 p.

Bogue, Margaret B. and Virginia A. Palmer. *Around the Shores of Lake Superior: A Guide to Historic Sites, Including a Color Tour Map Showing Lake Superior's Historic Sites.* Madison, Wis.: Univ. of Wis. Sea Grant College Program, 1979. 179 p.

Corbett, William P. "Pipestone: The Origin and Development of a National Monument," in *MH*, 47:83–92 (Fall, 1980).

Doermann, Elisabeth W. and Ellen M. Rosenthal. "Introducing the Hill House," in *MH*, 46:328–335 (Winter, 1979). The James J. Hill House, St. Paul.

Drake, Robert M. *The Minnesota Forest History Center.* Grand Rapids: Northprint Co., 1979. 31 p.

Eubank, Nancy. "Interpreting Historic Sites," in *MH*, 44:268–271 (Fall, 1975).

——. *The Lindberghs: Three Generations.* (Minn. Historic Sites Pamphlet Series 12.) St. Paul: MHS, 1975. 14 p. With bibliog.

Fridley, Russell W. "Acquiring Historic Sites: What Criteria?" in *MH*, 44:266–268 (Fall, 1975).

Hunt, Ron and Nancy Eubank. *A Living Past: 15 Historic Places in Minnesota.* Rev. ed. St. Paul: MHS, 1978. 30 p. 1st ed. published 1973.

Kandiyohi County Historical Society. *A Guide to Historical Sites in Kandiyohi County, Minnesota.* Willmar, [1966?]. 19 p. Reissued in shortened form as *A Guide to Historical Sites in Kandiyohi County*, [1971?].

Lamppa, Marvin. *A Report to the Department of Natural Resources on the Historical Aspects of the Vermilion, Cuyuna, and Mesabi Iron Ranges of Northeast Minnesota.* N.p.: [Dept. of Natural Resources?], 1977. 97 p.

Lofstrom, Ted and Lynne V. Spaeth. *Carver County: A Guide to Its Historic and Prehistoric Places.* St. Paul: MHS, 1978. 133 p. With bibliog.

Minnesota Historical Society. *A Historic Interpretation Program for the State of Minnesota: A Report Submitted to the Legislative Commission on Minnesota Resources.* St. Paul, 1977. 147 p.

——. *Minnesota Inventory of Historic and Prehistoric Places (Historic Preservation in Minnesota).* St. Paul, 1975. 96 p.

Nason, Wehrman, Chapman Associates, Inc. *Connor's Fur Post: Historic Site Development.* Minneapolis, [1976?]. 26 p.

Nordeen, Alcy B. and others. "Restoration of the Ard Godfrey House," in *Hennepin County History*, vol. 36, no. 2, 3, pp. 3–17 (Spring–Summer, 1977); vol. 38, no. 1, pp. 12–18, no. 4, pp. 13–23 (Spring, 1979, Winter, 1979–80). Minneapolis.

Skrief, Charles. *Historic Preservation for Minnesota Communities.* St. Paul: MHS State Historic Preservation Office and State Planning Agency, 1980. 64 p. Lists Minnesota sites on the National Register of Historic Places as of Feb., 1979.

Stillwater Bicentennial Commission, Tour Committee. *The Official Tour of Stillwater Historic Sites.* Rev. 2nd printing. Stillwater, 1978. 35 p.

Swanholm, Marx. "The Grand Mound Interpretive Center: Prehistory and the Public," in *Minnesota Archaeologist*, 37:84–95 (May, 1978).

Tegeder, Robert M. *Rediscovery and Restoration of Fort St. Charles.* [Collegeville]: St. John's Abbey Press, 1979. 202 p.

Wetherill, Fred E. *Nicollet County Bicentennial Historical Markers and Other Historical Places.* St. Peter: Nicollet County Bankers Assn., 1976. 67 p. Illustrated.

Place Names

Hartley, Alan H. "The Expansion of Ojibway and French Place-Names into the Lake Superior Region in the Seventeenth Century," in *Names*, 28:43–68 (Mar., 1980).

Kaups, Matti. "Finnish Place Names as a Form of Ethnic Expression in the Middle West, 1880–1977," in *Finnish Americana*, 1:51–70 (1978), 2:28–49 (1979).

Svendsen, G. Rolf. "Schools by Name—Not by Number," in *Hennepin County History*, vol. 33, no. 3, pp. 3–13 (Summer, 1974). In Minneapolis.

Woolworth, Alan R. "Indian Place Names of the Minnesota Region," in *Minnesota Archaeologist*, 35:3–12 (Dec., 1976). Largely bibliographical.

GEOLOGY AND GEOGRAPHY

Geology

Bray, Edmund C. *Billions of Years in Minnesota: The Geological Story of the State.* St. Paul: Science Museum, 1977. 102 p. With bibliog. Part 3 is a revision of *A Million Years in Minnesota*. St. Paul: Science Museum, 1962. 49 p.

Diedrick, Raymond T. and Richard H. Rust. "Glacial Lake Evidence in Western Minnesota as Interpreted from the Soil Survey," in Minn. Academy of Science, *Journal*, 41:9–12 (1975). Glacial Lake Benson.

Gruner, John W. *The Mineralogy and Geology of the Taconites and Iron Ores of the Mesabi Range, Minnesota.* St. Paul: Office of the Commissioner of Iron Range Resources and Rehabilitation, 1946. 127 p. With bibliog.

Hess, Jeffrey A. "The Riddle of the Land," in *Roots*, vol. 7, no. 3 (Spring, 1979). 31 p.

Schwartz, George M. *History of the Minnesota Geological Survey, With a Chapter on the Present Period by P. K. Sims.* (Minn. Geological Survey, Special Pub. 1.) Minneapolis, 1964. 39 p. With bibliog. of the publications of the Geological and Natural History Survey.

Wright, H. E., Jr., and William A. Watts. *Glacial and Vegetational History of Northeastern Minnesota.* (Minn. Geological Survey, Special Pub. 11.) Minneapolis, 1969. 59 p. With bibliog.

Geography

MAPS AND BOUNDARIES

Lass, William E. "How the Forty-Ninth Parallel Became the International Boundary," in *MH*, 44:209–219 (Summer, 1975).

———. *Minnesota's Boundary with Canada: Its Evolution Since 1783.* St. Paul: MHS, 1980. 141 p. With bibliog.

Lewis, G. Malcolm. "Changing National Perspectives and the Mapping of the Great Lakes between 1755 and 1795," in *Cartographica*, vol. 17, no. 3, pp. 1–31 (Autumn, 1980).

Seidl, Joan. "Minnesota Boundaries," in *Roots*, vol. 6, no. 2 (Winter, 1978). 31 p.

LAKES AND RIVERS

Adamson, Wendy W. *Who Owns a River? A Story of Environmental Action.* Minneapolis: Dillon, 1977. 95 p. With bibliog. The St. Croix.

Bradbury, John P. and Jean C. B. Waddington. "The Impact of European Settlement on Shagawa Lake, Northeastern Minnesota, U.S.A.," in H. J. B. Birks and Richard G. West, eds., *Quaternary Plant Ecology.* Oxford, Eng.: Blackwell, 1973, pp. 289–307. With bibliog. Ely area.

Lund, Duane R. *Lake of the Woods, Yesterday and Today.* Staples: Nordell Graphic Communications, 1975. 109 p. With bibliog.

———. *Tales of Four Lakes: Leech Lake, Gull Lake, Mille Lacs Lake, the Red Lakes, & the Crow Wing River.* Staples: Nordell Graphic Communications, 1977. 116 p.

Minnesota Dept. of Conservation, Div. of Waters. *Hydrologic Atlas of Minnesota.* (Bulletin 10.) St. Paul, 1959. [192] p. With bibliogs.

Waters, Thomas F. *The Streams and Rivers of Minnesota.* Minneapolis: Univ. of Minn. Press, 1977. 373 p. With bibliog.

NATURAL HISTORY AND CONSERVATION

Heinselman, M[iron] L. and H. C. Johnson. *Outline History of the BWCA.* N.p.: Friends of the Boundary Waters Wilderness, 1976. [4] p. Chronology.

"People, Places, and Things in Harmony," in *Roots*, vol. 1, no. 2 (Winter, 1973). 32 p.

Searle, R. Newell and Mark E. Heitlinger. *Prairies, Woods and Islands: A Guide to the Minnesota Preserves of the Nature Conservancy.* Minneapolis: Minn. Chapter, The Nature Conservancy, 1980. 73 p.

Flora and Fauna

Bolen, Don. *The Ballad of Ragnvald Sue.* Two Harbors: Privately published, 1978. 50 p. Commercial fishing.

Comeaux, Malcolm L. "Origin and Evolution of Mississippi River Fishing Craft," in *Pioneer America*, 10: 72–97 (June, 1978). With bibliog. Commercial fishing.

Eddy, Samuel and James C. Underhill. *Northern Fishes, with Special Reference to the Upper Mississippi Valley.* Rev. 3rd ed. Minneapolis: Univ. of Minn. Press,

1974. 414 p. With bibliog. 1st ed., by Eddy and Thaddeus Surber, published 1943.

Green, Janet C. and Robert B. Janssen. *Minnesota Birds: Where, When, and How Many*. Minneapolis: Univ. of Minn. Press, 1975. 217 p. With bibliog.

Kaups, Matti. "Evolution of Smelt-O-Mania on Lake Superior's North Shore," in *Journal of Popular Culture*, 11:959–976 (Spring, 1978).

———. "North Shore Commercial Fishing, 1849–1870," in *MH*, 46:42–58 (Summer, 1978).

Robinson, Jimmy. *The Best of Jimmy Robinson*. Detroit Lakes: Lakes Pub. Co., 1980. 334 p. Sports writer, hunter, and conservationist.

Schels, Carl. *I Lived to Tell the Story*. Elm Grove, Wis.: Sycamore Press, 1976. 212 p. Trapping and logging in the 1930s.

Swanson, Gustav and others. *The Mammals of Minnesota*. (Minn. Dept. of Conservation, Div. of Game and Fish, Technical Bull. 2.) St. Paul, 1945. 108 p.

U.S. Dept. of Agriculture, Soil Conservation Service. *Key to the Native Perennial Grasses: Midwest Region East of the Great Plains*. Washington: GPO, 1968. 116 p. Abstracted from Albert S. Hitchcock, *Manual of the Grasses*, 1950.

Wright, H. E., Jr. "The Roles of Pine and Spruce in the Forest History of Minnesota and Adjacent Areas," in *Ecology*, 49:937–955 (Summer, 1968). With bibliog.

State Parks

Eliseuson, Michael. *Tower Soudan—The State Park Down Under*. (Minn. State Park Heritage Series 1.) [St. Paul?]: Minn. Parks Foundation, 1976. 36 p. With bibliog.

Meyer, Roy W. "Forestville: The Making of a State Park," in *MH*, 44:82–95 (Fall, 1974).

Minnesota Dept. of Conservation, Div. of State Parks. *Minnesota State Parks, Memorials, Recreational Reserves, Waysides and Monuments*. St. Paul, 1955. 50 p. 1st published as *Minnesota State Parks and Monuments*, 1932.

Treuer, Robert. *Voyageur Country: A Park in the Wilderness*. Minneapolis: Univ. of Minn. Press, 1979. 173 p. With bibliog. Voyageurs National Park.

Forests and Forestry

Bachmann, Elizabeth M. *A History of Forestry in Minnesota: with Particular Reference to Forestry Legislation*. St. Paul: Minn. Dept. of Conservation, Div. of Forestry, 1965. 109 p. With bibliog. An abridged version without bibliog. is in *Conservation Volunteer*, July, 1960–May, 1961. Reprinted with additions by Assn. of Minn. Div. of Lands and Forestry Employees, 1969.

Chapman, Herman H. *A Historic Record of Development of Quetico-Superior Wilderness Area and of the Chippewa National Forest, Minnesota*. N.p.: Privately published, [1957?]. 35 p. With bibliog.

Searle, R. Newell. "Minnesota Forestry Comes of Age: Christopher C. Andrews, 1895–1911," in *Forest History*, 17:14–25 (July, 1973).

———. "Minnesota State Forestry Association: Seedbed of Forest Conservation," in *MH*, 44:16–29 (Spring, 1974).

CLIMATE

Brinkmann, Waltraud A. R. "Lake Superior Area Temperature Variations," in Assn. of Am. Geographers, *Annals*, 70:17–30 (1980).

Pine, Carol. *Life on the Line, An NSP Documentary: The Storm of the Century, January 10–12, 1975*. Minneapolis: Northern States Power Co., 1975. 109 p.

Rossman, George and others. *Water and Weather in North Central Minnesota*. Grand Rapids: Northprint Co., 1976. 23 p. With bibliog. Grand Rapids area.

U.S. Environmental Data Service. *Climates of the States: Climate of Minnesota*. (Climatography of the United States 60–21.) By Earl L. Kuehnast. Washington, 1972. 20 p. With bibliog. First published by U.S. Weather Bureau, 1959.

Floods

Anderson, David B. and Harlan H. Schwob. *Floods of April–May 1969 in Upper Midwestern United States: Open-File Report*. St. Paul: U.S. Dept. of the Interior, Geological Survey, Water Resources Div., 1970. 555 p. With bibliog.

Hurst, W. D. "The Red River Flood of 1950," in Historical and Scientific Soc. of Manitoba, *Papers*, 3rd series, 12:55–84 (1957).

Matheson, S. P. "Floods at Red River," in Historical and Scientific Soc. of Manitoba, *Papers*, 3rd series, 3:5–13 (1947). The floods of 1826, 1852, and 1861.

INDIANS
General

Archabal, Nina M. "Frances Densmore: Pioneer in the Study of American Indian Music," in Barbara Stuhler and Gretchen Kreuter, eds., *Women of Minnesota: Selected Biographical Essays*. St. Paul: MHS, 1977, pp. 94–115.

Bonney, Rachel A. "The Role of AIM Leaders in Indian Nationalism," in *American Indian Quarterly*, 3:209–224 (Autumn, 1977). American Indian Movement founded in Minneapolis in 1968.

Densmore, Frances. *Dakota and Ojibwe People in Minnesota*. St. Paul: MHS, 1977. 55 p. First published as

Roots, vol. 5, nos. 2, 3 (Winter, Spring, 1977). Written for children.

Foster, J. E. "The Métis: The People and the Term," in *Prairie Forum*, vol. 3, no. 1, pp. 79–90 (1978).

Hofmann, Charles, comp. and ed. *Frances Densmore and American Indian Music: A Memorial Volume.* (Contributions from the Museum of the Am. Indian Heye Foundation 23.) New York: The Foundation, 1968. 127 p. Contains some of Densmore's lectures, reports, articles, and personal papers.

Katz, Jane, ed. *This Song Remembers: Self Portraits of Native Americans in the Arts.* Boston: Houghton Mifflin Co., 1980. 207 p. George Morrison, pp. 53–60; Amos Owen, pp. 64–70; Gerald Vizenor, pp. 163–169.

Manypenny, George W. *Our Indian Wards.* Cincinnati: R. Clarke & Co., 1880. 436 p. Reprinted, New York: Da Capo Press, 1972.

Peterson, Jacqueline. "Prelude to Red River: A Social Portrait of the Great Lakes Métis," in *Ethnohistory*, 25:41–67 (Winter, 1978). Green Bay, Wis., métis and relations to the Red River métis people.

Quimby, George I. *Indian Culture and European Trade Goods: The Archaeology of the Historic Period in the Western Great Lakes Region.* Madison: Univ. of Wisconsin Press, 1966. 217 p.

Raygor, Mearl W. *Indians of Southeastern Minnesota.* N.p.: Privately published, 1978. 36 p.

Science Museum of Minnesota. *Straight Tongue: Minnesota Indian Art from the Bishop Whipple Collections.* St. Paul, 1980. 91 p. With bibliog. Exhibit catalog.

Smith, G. Hubert. "Ethnographic Contributions of J. N. Nicollet," in *Minnesota Archaeologist*, 36:61–75 (July, 1977).

Sorkin, Alan L. *The Urban American Indian.* Lexington, Mass.: Lexington Books, 1978. 158 p. Minneapolis, *passim.*

Thornton, Russell and Mary K. Grasmick. *Bibliography of Social Science Research and Writings on American Indians.* Minneapolis: Center for Urban and Regional Affairs, Univ. of Minn., 1979. 160 p. Journal articles, mostly from history journals, but including political science, geography, economics, ethnic studies, and sociology.

Prehistory

Anfinson, Scott F. and others. *The Lake Bronson Site (21 KT 1): A Multi-Component Prehistoric Site on the Prairie-Woodland Border in Northwestern Minnesota.* (Occasional Publications in Minn. Anthropology 3.) St. Paul: Minn. Archaeological Soc., 1978. 60 p.

Benn, David W. "Some Trends and Traditions in Woodland Cultures of the Quad-State Region in the Upper Mississippi River Basin," in *Wisconsin Archeologist*, new series, 60:47–82 (Mar., 1979).

Birk, Douglas A. "The Norway Lake Site: A Multicomponent Woodland Complex in North Central Minnesota," in *Minnesota Archaeologist*, 36:16–45 (Feb., 1977). Cass County.

———. *The Survey of Grey Cloud Island, Washington County, Minnesota: An Archaeological Approach.* St. Paul: MHS, 1972. 102 p. With bibliogs. Reprinted in *Minnesota Archaeologist*, vol. 32, nos. 1, 2, pp. 1–102 (1973).

——— and Douglas C. George. "A Woodland Survey Strategy and its Application in the Salvage of a Late Archaic Locus of the Smith Mounds Site, (21 KC 3), Koochiching County, Minnesota," in *Minnesota Archaeologist*. 35:[ii], 1–30 (Nov., 1976).

Caine, Christy A. H. and T. Allen Caine. "The Clarence Currie Collection from St. Croix State Park, Minnesota," in *Wisconsin Archeologist*, new series, 53: 70–75 (June, 1972).

Doermann, Elisabeth. "Early Indian People," in *Roots*, vol. 7, no. 2 (Winter, 1979). 31 p.

Gibbon, Guy. "The Brower Site: A Middle Woodland Mound and Camp Site of Lake Onamia," in *Minnesota Archaeologist*, 34:1–43 (1975).

———. "The Crace Site: A Late Woodland Special Activity Site on Lake Onamia," in *Minnesota Archaeologist*, 34:49–70 (1975).

———. *The Mississippian Occupation of the Red Wing Area.* (Minn. Prehistoric Archaeology Series 13.) St. Paul: MHS, 1979. 394 p. on 5 microfiche cards.

———. "The Old Shakopee Bridge Site: A Late Woodland Ricing Site on Shakopee Lake, Mille Lacs County, Minnesota," in *Minnesota Archaeologist*, 35: 2–56 (1976).

Hudson, Lew. "Blue Mounds' Stone Fence," in *Minnesota Archaeologist*, 37:50–55 (May, 1978). Includes a letter from Frederick Manfred.

———. "Major Prehistoric Site Found," in *Minnesota Archaeologist*, 38:199–205 (Nov., 1979). First published in *Worthington Daily Globe*, Aug. 10, 11, 1977. Yellow Medicine County.

———. "State's Oldest Dwelling Found Near Mountain Lake," in *Minnesota Archaeologist*, 38:26–31 (1979). First published in *Worthington Daily Globe*, July 10, 1976. Cottonwood County.

———. *The Wolff Mound.* Worthington: Sioux Archaeological Soc., 1974. 44 p.

Johnson, Elden. *The Prehistoric Peoples of Minnesota.* Rev. 2nd ed. (Minn. Prehistoric Archaeology Series 3.) St. Paul: MHS, 1978. 30 p. With bibliog. 1st ed. published 1969.

———, ed. *Aspects of Upper Great Lakes Anthropology: Papers in Honor of Lloyd A. Wilford.* (Minn. Prehistoric Archaeology Series 11.) St. Paul: MHS, 1974. 200 p. With bibliog. Includes "Lloyd A. Wilford and Minnesota Archaeology," pp. 1–7; H. E. Wright,

Jr., "The Environment of Early Man in the Great Lakes Region," pp. 8–14; Nancy S. Ossenberg, "Origins and Relationships of Woodland Peoples: The Evidence of Cranial Morphology," pp. 15–39; Christy A. H. Caine, "The Archaeology of the Snake River Region in Minnesota," pp. 55–63; Jack Steinbring, "The Preceramic Archaeology of Northern Minnesota," pp. 64–73; James B. Stoltman, "Within–Laurel Cultural Variability in Northern Minnesota," pp. 74–89; Guy E. Gibbon, "A Model of Mississippian Development and Its Implications for the Red Wing Area," pp. 129–137; Charles R. Watrall, "Subsistence Pattern Change at the Cambria Site: A Review and Hypothesis," pp. 138–142; Mildred M. Wedel, "Le Sueur and the Dakota Sioux," pp. 157–171.

Lass, Barbara. "Radiocarbon Dates from Minnesota Archaeological Sites to 1979," in *Minnesota Archaeologist*, 39:29–39 (Feb., 1980).

Lawrence, Donald B. and Makarand Jawadekar. "Some Aboriginal Minnesota Names Borrowed from Sanskrit and Japanese," in Minn. Academy of Science, *Journal*, 45:14–17 (Spring, 1979).

Link, Adolph W. "Chunkey: The Game and Its Probable Use by Mississippians in Minnesota," in *Minnesota Archaeologist*, 38:129–145 (Aug., 1979).

Lothson, Gordon A. *The Jeffers Petroglyphs Site: A Survey and Analysis of the Carvings.* (Minn. Prehistoric Archaeology Series 12.) St. Paul: MHS, 1976. 52 p.

―――― and Nancy Eubank. *Jeffers Petroglyphs Walking Tour: A Journey through Time.* (Minn. Historic Sites Pamphlet Series 8.) St. Paul: MHS, 1974. 26 p.

Lugenbeal, Edward. "The Blackduck Ceramics of the Smith Site (21 KC 3) and Their Implications for the History of Blackduck Ceramics and Culture in Northern Minnesota," in *Midcontinental Journal of Archaeology*, 3:45–68 (Spring, 1978).

Michlovic, Michael G. *The Dead River Site (21 OT 51).* (Occasional Publications in Minn. Anthropology 6.) St. Paul: Minn. Archaeological Soc., 1979. 39 p. With bibliog. Otter Tail County.

―――― and others. "Is North Arvilla Ancestral Cheyenne?" in *Minnesota Archaeologist*, 36:155–160 (Dec., 1977).

Minnesota Archaeologist. Published by the Minnesota Archaeological Soc., Minneapolis, later St. Paul, monthly from June 1, 1935, through Sept., 1938; quarterly from Apr., 1939; with brief suspensions. Contains many pertinent articles not listed in this bibliog. Subject and author indexes to vols. 1–33 (1933–74) in 33, nos. 3, 4, pp. 36–90 (1974) to vols. 34–38 (1975–79) in 39, no. 1, pp. 40–50 (Feb., 1980).

Neumann, Thomas W. and Elden Johnson. "Patrow Site Lithic Analysis," in *Midcontinental Journal of Archaeology*, 4:79–111 (1979). Itasca County.

Obey, Wilda A. "The Arvilla People," in *Minnesota Archaeologist*, 33:1–33 (1974).

Oothoudt, Jerry W. "Petrified Indian Cave: The Legend and the Archaeology," in *Minnesota Archaeologist*, 38:161–178 (Nov., 1979). Fillmore County.

―――― and Clifford W. Watson. "The Hyland Lake Island Site (21 HE 31): A Unique Opportunity in Hennepin County," in *Minnesota Archaeologist*, 37:125–148 (Aug., 1978).

Peterson, Leslie D. "An Early Prehistoric Stone Workshop Site in Northwestern Minnesota," in *Minnesota Archaeologist*, vol. 32, nos. 3, 4, pp. 1–57 (1973). Greenbush site, Roseau County.

―――― and Scott F. Anfinson. "Minnesota's Highway Archeology Program," in *Minnesota Archaeologist*, 38:86–102 (May, 1979).

Shay, C. Thomas. "Bison Procurement on the Eastern Margin of the Plains: The Itasca Site," in *Plains Anthropologist*, Nov., 1978, pp. 140–150. Clearwater County.

Swanholm, Marx. *Shadows in the Stillness: Early Man on the Rainy River.* (Minn. Historic Sites Pamphlet Series 16.) St. Paul: MHS, 1978. 24 p. With bibliog.

Syms, Leigh. "The Devils Lake–Sourisford Burial Complex on the Northern Plains," in *Plains Anthropologist*, 24:283–308 (1979).

Wilford, Lloyd A. and John W. Brink. "Hogback: A Proto-Historic Oneota Burial Site," in *Minnesota Archaeologist*, 33:1–79 (1974). A site of the Iowa Indians in Houston County.

Woolworth, Alan R. and Mark A. Hall, eds. *Some Studies of Minnesota Prehistoric Ceramics: Papers Presented at the First Council for Minnesota Archaeology Symposium, 1976.* (Occasional Publications in Minn. Anthropology 2.) St. Paul: Minn. Archaeological Soc., 1978. 68 p.

Ojibway (Chippewa)

GENERAL

Armstrong, Benjamin G. "Reminiscences of Life Among the Chippewa," in *Wisconsin Magazine of History*, 55:175–196, 287–309, 56:37–58, 140–161 (Spring, 1972–Winter, 1972–73). First published as *Early Life Among the Indians.* Ashland, Wis.: Press of A. W. Bowron, 1892.

Benton–Banai, Edward. *The Mishomis Book: The Voice of the Ojibway.* St. Paul: Indian Country Press, 1979. 114 p. A retelling of the "Mishomis" or grandfather teachings.

Bibliography of Ojibwe Resource Materials. (Occasional Publications in Minn. Anthropology 8.) St. Paul: Minn. Archaeological Soc., 1981. 24 p. Originally comp. by MHS.

Bishop, Charles A. "The Emergence of the Northern Ojibwa: Social and Economic Consequences," in *American Ethnologist*, 3:39–54 (Feb., 1976).

Blessing, Fred K., Jr. *The Ojibway Indians Observed: Papers . . . on the Ojibway Indians, from* The Minnesota Archaeologist. (Occasional Publications in Minn. Anthropology 1.) St. Paul: Minn. Archaeological Soc., 1977. 259 p.

Brill, Charles. *Indian and Free: A Contemporary Portrait of Life on a Chippewa Reservation*. Minneapolis: Univ. of Minn. Press, 1974. 143 p. Red Lake Reservation, mainly photographs.

Bromley, Edward A. "Hole-in-the-Day, the Chippewa Chief; Why He Failed in 1862 to Capture Minneapolis and St. Paul," in *Minnesota Archaeologist*, 39:138–149 (Aug., 1980). Reprinted from *Minneapolis Times*, Sept. 12, 1897.

Copway, George. *Indian Life and Indian History by an Indian Author: Embracing the Traditions of the North American Indians Regarding Themselves, Particularly of that Most Important of All the Tribes, the Ojibways*. New York: AMS Press, 1978. 266 p. First published, Boston: Albert Colby Co., 1860.

Danziger, Edmund J., Jr. *The Chippewas of Lake Superior*. (Civilization of the Am. Indian 148.) Norman: Univ. of Oklahoma Press, 1978. 263 p. With bibliog.

Densmore, Frances. *Chippewa Customs*. (U.S. Bureau of Am. Ethnology, Bull. 86.) Washington: GPO, 1929. 204 p. Reprinted with new introd. by Nina M. Archabal. St. Paul: MHS, 1979.

———. "Uses of Plants by the Chippewa Indians," in U.S. Bureau of Am. Ethnology, *Annual Report* [1926–27], 44:275–397 (1928). Reprinted as *How Indians Use Wild Plants for Food, Medicine and Crafts*. New York: Dover, 1974.

Des Jarlait, Patrick. *The Story of an American Indian Artist, as Told to Neva Williams*. Minneapolis: Lerner, 1975. 57 p.

Gilman, Carolyn. "Chippewa Customs: The Collection of Frances Densmore," in *Minnesota Archaeologist*, 39:3–16 (Feb., 1980).

Hickerson, Harold. *Ethnohistory of Chippewa in Central Minnesota*. (Am. Indian Ethnohistory, North Central and Northeastern Indians, Chippewa Indians 4.) New York: Garland Pub. Co., 1974. 253 p.

———. *Ethnohistory of Chippewa of Lake Superior*; [and] Helen E. Knuth, *Economic and Historical Background of Northeastern Minnesota Lands: Chippewa Indians of Lake Superior*. (Am. Indian Ethnohistory, North Central and Northeastern Indians, Chippewa Indians 3.) New York: Garland Pub. Co., 1970. 295 p. With bibliog.

———. *Ethnohistory of Mississippi Bands and Pillager and Winnebigoshish Bands of Chippewa*. (Am. Indian Ethnohistory, North Central and Northeastern Indians, Chippewa Indians 2.) New York: Garland Pub. Co., 1974. 317 p. With bibliog.

Hilger, Sister Inez. *Chippewa Child Life and Its Cultural Background*. (U.S. Bureau of Am. Ethnology, Bull. 146.) Washington: GPO, 1951. 204 p. With bibliog. Reprinted, New York: AMS Press, 1979.

———. *A Social Study of One Hundred Fifty Chippewa Indian Families of the White Earth Reservation of Minnesota*. Washington: Catholic Univ. of Am. Press, 1939. 251 p. Reprinted, New York: AMS Press, 1980. With bibliog.

Kegg, Maude. *Gabekanaansing/At the End of the Trail: Memories of Chippewa Childhood in Minnesota, with Texts in Ojibwe and English*. Ed. and transcribed by John Nichols. Thunder Bay, Ont.: Privately published, 1978. 85 p.

Kvasnicka, Robert M. "From the Wilderness to Washington—and Back Again: The Story of the Chippewa Delegation of 1855," in *Kansas Quarterly*, 3:56–63 (Fall, 1971).

Loftus, Michael K. "A Late Historic Period Chippewa Sugar Maple Camp," in *Wisconsin Archeologist*, new series, 58:71–76 (Mar., 1977). At Hoyt Lakes.

Minnesota Chippewa Tribe. *Minnesota Chippewa Tribal Government: Student Handbook*. Bemidji: Pioneer, 1978. 201 p. Federal policy.

Paredes, J. Anthony, ed. *Anishinabe: 6 Studies of Modern Chippewa*. Tallahassee: Univ. Presses of Florida, 1980. 436 p. With bibliog.

Ritzenthaler, Robert E. and Pat Ritzenthaler. *The Woodland Indians of the Western Great Lakes*. Garden City, N.Y.: Am. Museum of Natural History, 1970. 178 p. Culture.

Rogers, John (Chief Snow Cloud). *Red World and White: Memories of a Chippewa Boyhood*. Norman: Univ. of Oklahoma Press, 1974. xvii, 153 p. First published as *A Chippewa Speaks*, 1957.

Rogers, Virginia. "The Indians and the Métis: Genealogical Sources on Minnesota's Earliest Settlers," in *MH*, 46:286–295 (Fall, 1979).

Roufs, Timothy G. *The Anishinabe of the Minnesota Chippewa Tribe*. Phoenix, Ariz.: Indian Tribal Series, 1975. 104 p.

———. "Early Indian Life in the Lake Superior Region," in *Minnesota Archaeologist*, 37:157–196 (Nov., 1978).

Smith, James G. E. "Proscription of Cross–Cousin Marriage among the Southwestern Ojibwa," in *American Ethnologist*, 1:751–762 (Nov., 1974).

Tanner, Helen H. *The Ojibwas: A Critical Bibliography*. (Newberry Library Center for the History of the Am. Indian, Bibliographical Series.) Bloomington: Indiana Univ. Press, 1976. 78 p.

U.S. Indian Claims Commission. *Commission Findings on the Chippewa Indians*. (Am. Indian Ethnohistory,

North Central and Northeastern Indians, Chippewa Indians 7.) New York: Garland Pub. Co., 1974. 548 p.

Wheeler-Voegelin, Erminie and Harold Hickerson. *The Red Lake and Pembina Chippewa.* (Am. Indian Ethnohistory, North Central and Northeastern Indians, Chippewa Indians 1.) New York: Garland Pub. Co., 1974. 230 p. With bibliog.

Woolworth, Nancy L. "Miss Densmore Meets the Ojibwe: Frances Densmore's Ethnomusicology Studies among the Grand Portage Ojibwe in 1905," in *Minnesota Archaeologist*, 38:106–134 (Aug., 1979).

Zapffe, Carl A. *The Man Who Lived in 3 Centuries: A Biographic Reconstruction of the Life of Kahbe nagwi wens, a Native Minnesotan.* Brainerd: Historic Heartland, 1975. 96 p. With bibliog. Also known as John Smith.

RELIGION

Dewdney, Selwyn. *The Sacred Scrolls of the Southern Ojibway.* Toronto: Univ. of Toronto Press, published for the Glenbow–Alberta Institute, Calgary, Alta., 1975. 199 p. Illustrations.

Róhrl, Vivian. "Some Observations on the Drum Society of Chippewa Indians," in *Ethnohistory*, 19:219–225 (Summer, 1972). Mille Lacs Lake Reservation.

Vennum, Thomas, Jr. "Ojibwa Origin–Migration Songs of the *mitewiwin*," in *Journal of American Folklore*, 91:753–791 (July–Sept., 1978). White Earth and Mille Lacs Lake reservations.

Dakota (Sioux)
GENERAL

Anderson, Gary C. "Early Dakota Migration and Intertribal War: A Revision," in *Western Historical Quarterly*, 11:17–36 (Jan., 1980).

Copeland, Marion W. *Charles Alexander Eastman (Ohiyesa).* (Boise State Univ. Western Writers Series 33.) Boise State Univ., 1978. 43 p.

Eastman, Charles A. *Indian Boyhood.* New York: Phillips & Co., 1902. 289 p. Reprinted, New York: Dover, 1971. 245 p.

Eastman, Elaine G. *Sister to the Sioux: The Memoirs of Elaine Goodale Eastman, 1885–91.* Ed. by Kay Graber. Lincoln: Univ. of Nebraska Press, 1978. 175 p. Teacher in South Dakota and wife of Charles A. Eastman.

Eastman, Mary. *Dahcotah; or, Life and Legends of the Sioux around Fort Snelling.* New York: John Wiley, 1849. 268 p. Reprinted, Minneapolis: Ross & Haines, 1962; New York: Arno Press, 1975.

Hanson, James A. *Metal Weapons, Tools, and Ornaments of the Teton Dakota Indians.* Lincoln: Univ. of Nebraska Press, 1975. 118 p. With bibliog. Illustrations.

Hickerson, Harold. *Mdewakanton Band of Sioux Indians.* (Am. Indian Ethnohistory, Plains Indians, Sioux Indians 1.) New York: Garland Pub. Co., 1974. 303 p. With bibliog.

Hoover, Herbert T. *The Sioux: A Critical Bibliography.* Bloomington: Indiana Univ. Press, 1979. 78 p.

Howard, James H. "Some Further Thoughts on Eastern Dakota 'Clans'," in *Ethnohistory*, 26:133–140 (Spring, 1979).

Jacobson, Clair. "A History of the Yanktonai and Hunkpatina Sioux," in *North Dakota History*, vol. 47, no. 1, pp. 4–24 (Winter, 1980).

Lee, Betsy. *Charles Eastman.* Minneapolis: Dillon Press, 1979. 62 p.

Lettermann, Edward J. *From Whole Log to No Log: A History of the Indians Where the Mississippi and the Minnesota Rivers Meet.* Minneapolis: Dillon Press, 1969. 291 p. With bibliog.

Marken, Jack W. and Herbert T. Hoover. *Bibliography of the Sioux.* (Native Am. Bibliography Series.) Metuchen, N.J.: Scarecrow Press, 1980. 388 p.

Meyer, Roy W. *History of the Santee Sioux: United States Indian Policy on Trial.* Lincoln: Univ. of Nebraska Press, 1967. 434 p. Reprinted, Lincoln: Bison Books, 1980.

Paulson, Howard W. "The Allotment of Land in Severalty to the Dakota Indians before the Dawes Act," in *South Dakota History*, 1:132–153 (Spring, 1971).

Sibley, Henry H. "Sport of Buffalo Hunting on the Open Plains of Pembina," in *Minnesota Archaeologist*, 39:177–198 (Dec., 1980). First published in Henry R. Schoolcraft, ed. *Historical and Statistical Information Respecting the History, Condition, and Prospects of the Indian Tribes of the United States*, 1854. Vol. 4, pp. 94–110.

Stensland, Anna L. "Charles Alexander Eastman: Sioux Storyteller and Historian," in *American Indian Quarterly*, 3:199–208 (Autumn, 1977).

Textor, Lucy E. *Official Relations between the United States and the Sioux Indians.* (Leland Stanford, Jr. Univ. Publications, History and Economics 2.) Palo Alto, Calif., 1896. Sioux of the Mississippi, pp. 56–94.

U.S. Indian Claims Commission. *Commission Findings on the Sioux Indians.* (Am. Indian Ethnohistory, Plains Indians, Sioux Indians 4.) New York: Garland Pub. Co., 1974. 360 p.

Werner, Reinhold O. *Burial Places of the Aborigines of Kaposia.* N.p.: Kaposia Press, 1974. 10 p.

Wilson, Raymond. "The Writings of Ohiyesa—Charles Alexander Eastman, M.D., Santee Sioux," in *South Dakota History*, 6:55–73 (Winter, 1975).

Winchell, Newton H. "Habitations of the Sioux in Minnesota," in *Minnesota Archeologist*, 38:18–25 (Feb., 1979). First published in *Wisconsin Archeologist*, 7:155–164 (1906).

Woolworth, Alan R. *Ethnohistorical Report on the Yankton Sioux.* (Am. Indian Ethnohistory, Plains Indians, Sioux Indians 3.) New York: Garland Pub. Co., 1974. 245 p. With bibliog.

———— and Nancy L. Woolworth. "Eastern Dakota Settlement and Subsistence Patterns Prior to 1851," in *Minnesota Archaeologist*, 39:70–89 (May, 1980).

Wozniak, John S. *Contact, Negotiation and Conflict: An Ethnohistory of the Eastern Dakota, 1819–1839.* Washington: Univ. Press of America, 1978. 148 p. With bibliog.

DAKOTA WAR, 1862

Carley, Kenneth. *The Sioux Uprising of 1862.* 2nd ed. St. Paul: MHS, 1976. 102 p. 1st ed. published 1961. With bibliog.

Dietz, Charlton. "Henry Behnke: New Ulm's Paul Revere," in *MH*, 45:111–115 (Fall, 1976).

Henig, Gerald S. "A Neglected Cause of the Sioux Uprising," in *MH*, 45:107–110 (Fall, 1976).

Nichols, David A. *Lincoln and the Indians: Civil War Policy and Politics.* Columbia: Univ. of Missouri Press, 1978. Sioux Uprising and Bishop Whipple's activities, pp. 65–160.

————. "The Other Civil War: Lincoln and the Indians," in *MH*, 44:2–15 (Spring, 1974).

Nicolay, John G. "The Sioux War," in *Minnesota Archaeologist*, 38:179–189 (Nov., 1979). First published in *Continental Monthly*, 3:195–204 (Feb., 1863), and reprinted in Theodore C. Blegen, ed., *Lincoln's Secretary Goes West: Two Reports by John G. Nicolay on Frontier Indian Troubles, 1862.* La Crosse, Wis.: Sumac Press, 1965, pp. 45–69.

Noyes, Edward. "Neighbors 'To the Rescue': Wisconsin and Iowa Troops Fight Boredom, Not Indians, in Minnesota in 1862," in *MH*, 46:312–327 (Winter, 1979).

Robertson, Thomas A. "Reminiscence," in *South Dakota Historical Collections*, 20:559–601 (1940).

Russo, Priscilla A. "The Time to Speak is Over: The Onset of the Sioux Uprising," in *MH*, 45:97–106 (Fall, 1976).

Sully, Langdon. *No Tears for the General: The Life of Alfred Sully, 1821–1879.* Palo Alto, Calif.: American West Pub. Co., 1974. "The Great Sioux Uprising," pp. 162–179.

Aftermath

[Daniels, Arthur M.]. *A Journal of Sibley's Indian Expedition During the Summer of 1863 and Record of the Troops Employed.* Minneapolis: James D. Thueson, Publisher, 1980. 154 p. First published, Winona Republican, 1864.

Jacobson, Clair. "The Battle of Whitestone Hill [Dakota Territory]," in *North Dakota History*, 44:4–14 (Summer, 1977).

Krause, Herbert and Gary D. Olson. *Prelude to Glory: A Newspaper Accounting of Custer's 1874 Expedition to the Black Hills.* Sioux Falls, S.D.: Brevet Press, 1974. Involvement of William H. Illingworth, photographer, and St. Paul newspapers, pp. 33–35, 39, 40, 79, 80.

Laviolette, Gontran. *The Sioux Indians in Canada.* Regina, Sask.: Marian Press, 1944. 138 p. With bibliog.

McKusick, Marshall B. *The Iowa Northern Border Brigade.* (Office of State Archaeologist, Report 8.) Iowa City, 1975. 172 p. With bibliog.

Stuart, Paul. *History of the Flandreau Santee Sioux Tribe.* Flandreau, S.D.: Tribal History Program, Flandreau Santee Sioux Tribe, 1971. 194 p.

Treaties, Indian Agents, and Indian Medals

Danziger, Edmund J., Jr. "They Would Not Be Moved: The Chippewa Treaty of 1854," in *MH*, 43:175–185 (Spring, 1973).

Gilman, Carolyn. "Grand Portage Ojibway Indians Give British Medals to Historical Society," in *MH*, 47:26–32 (Spring, 1980).

Hoover, Herbert T. "Yankton Sioux Tribal Claims Against the United States, 1917–1975," in *Western Historical Quarterly*, 7:125–142 (Apr., 1976).

Keller, Robert H., Jr. "On Teaching Indian History: Legal Jurisdiction in Chippewa Treaties," in *Ethnohistory*, 19:209–218 (Summer, 1972).

Kvasnicka, Robert M. and Herman J. Viola, eds. *The Commissioners of Indian Affairs, 1824–1977.* Lincoln: Univ. of Nebraska Press, 1979. 384 p. Minn., *passim*. Biographies of the commissioners.

Newcombe, Barbarba T. " 'A Portion of the American People': The Sioux Sign a Treaty in Washington in 1858," in *MH*, 45:82–96 (Fall, 1976).

Pfaller, Louis L. *James McLaughlin: The Man with an Indian Heart.* New York: Vantage Press, 1978. Minn. episodes, pp. 1–15, 234–238, 291–297.

Missions and Missionaries

Bigglestone, William E. "Oberlin College and the Beginning of the Red Lake Mission," in *MH*, 45:21–31 (Spring, 1976).

Norton, Sister Mary Aquinas. *Catholic Missionary Activities in the Northwest, 1818–1864.* Washington: Catholic Univ. of America, 1930. 154 p. With bibliog.

Provencher, Joseph N. "Memoir or Account of the Establishment of the Red River Mission, and Its Progress since 1818. Presented to the Propaganda, March 12, 1836," ed. by J. E. Rea, in *The Beaver*, 303:16–23 (Spring, 1973).

EXPLORATION AND DISCOVERY

General

"Exploration," in *Roots*, vol. 4, no. 3 (Spring, 1976). 31 p. Includes French, British, and American explorers.

Trewartha, Glenn T. "Population and Settlements in the Upper Mississippi Hill Land during the Period of Destructive Exploitation (1670–1832)," in Eighth Am. Scientific Congress, *Proceedings*, 183–196 (1943). Includes southeastern Minn.

———. "A Second Epoch of Destructive Occupance in the Driftless Hill Land (1760–1832)," in Assn. of Am. Geographers, *Annals*, 30:109–142 (June, 1940).

Kensington Rune Stone

"The Case of the Gran Tapes: Further Evidence on the Rune Stone Riddle," in *MH*, 45:152–156 (Winter, 1976). An interview of Walter Gran.

Fridley, Russell W. "Debate Continues over Kensington Rune Stone," in *MH*, 45:149–151 (Winter, 1976).

"More on the Rune Stone," in *MH*, 45:195–199 (Spring, 1977). Communications from readers.

Redmond, Jeffrey R. *"Viking" Hoaxes in North America*. New York: Carlton Press, 1979. The Kensington rune stone, pp. 25–30.

French Period

Crouse, Nellis M. *La Vérendrye: Fur Trader and Explorer*. Ithaca, N.Y.: Cornell Univ. Press, 1956. 247 p. Reprinted, Port Washington, N.Y.: Kennikat Press, 1972. With bibliog.

Dictionary of Canadian Biography. Vols. 1–4, 9, 10, and index. Univ. of Toronto Press, 1966–81. Contain authoritative, short biographies, with bibliogs., of the following travelers and explorers in the Minnesota country: Claude Allouez, Jean-Pierre Aulneau, René Boucher de La Perrière, Claude Dablon, Jean-Baptiste Gaultier de La Vérendrye, Louis-Joseph Gaultier de La Vérendrye, Pierre Gaultier de Varennes et de La Vérendrye, Claude Greysolon de La Tourette, Daniel Greysolon Dulhut, Médard Chouart des Groseilliers, Michel Guignas, Louis Hennepin, Joseph La France, Louis-Armand de Lom d'Arce de Lahontan, Pierre-Charles Le Sueur, Pierre-Esprit Radisson. Vols. 1–4, 9, 10, and index to vol. 1–4 only published so far.

Dunn, James T. "Du Luth's Birthplace: A Footnote to History," in *MH*, 46:228–232 (Summer, 1979).

Heidenreich, Conrad E. "Mapping the Great Lakes: The Period of Exploration, 1603–1700," in *Cartographica*, vol. 17, no. 3, pp. 32–64 (Autumn, 1980).

Johnston, Patricia C. "Portrayals of Hennepin, 'Discoverer' of the Falls of St. Anthony, 1680," in *MH*, 47:57–62 (Summer, 1980). Paintings and sculpture depicting Hennepin and his exploits.

Neill, Edward D. "The Development of Trade on Lake Superior and Its Tributaries during the French Regime," in *Macalester College Contributions*, 1:[77]–140 (1890).

Nute, Grace L. *Caesars of the Wilderness: Médard Chouart, Sieur des Groseilliers and Pierre Esprit Radisson, 1618–1710*. New York: Appleton–Century, 1943. 386 p. With bibliog. Reprinted, St. Paul: MHS, 1978, with introd. by Bruce M. White and additional map.

Smith, G. Hubert. *The Explorations of the La Vérendryes in the Northern Plains, 1738–43*. Ed. by W. Raymond Wood. Lincoln: Univ. of Nebraska Press, 1980. 160 p. With bibliog.

Sommer, Lawrence J., ed. *Daniel Greysolon, Sieur duLhut: A Tercentenary Tribute*. Duluth: St. Louis County Historical Soc., 1979. 24 p. With bibliog.

British Period

Carver, Jonathan. *The Journals of Jonathan Carver and Related Documents, 1766–1770*. Ed. by John Parker. St. Paul: MHS, 1976. 244 p. With bibliog. Includes James S. Goddard, "Journal of a Voyage, 1766–67," ed. by Carolyn Gilman, pp. 180–191.

Henry, Alexander, Sr. *Alexander Henry's Travels and Adventures in the Years 1760–1776*. Ed. with introd. by Milo M. Quaife. (Lakeside Classics.) Chicago: R. R. Donnelley, 1921. 340 p. 1st ed. published New York, 1809. Reprinted as *Travels and Adventures in Canada and the Indian Territories, 1760–1776*. New York: Garland Pub. Co., 1976.

Kellogg, Louise P. *The British Regime in Wisconsin and the Northwest*. Madison: State Historical Soc. of Wis., 1935. Reprinted, New York: Da Capo Press, 1972.

Woolworth, Nancy L. "Grand Portage in the Revolutionary War," in *MH*, 44:198–208 (Summer, 1975).

Nineteenth–Century Explorers

Bray, Martha C. *Joseph Nicollet and His Map*. Philadelphia: Am. Philosophical Soc., 1980. 300 p. With bibliog. Two folded maps included.

Friis, Herman R. "Stephen H. Long's Unpublished Map of the United States Compiled in 1820–1822 (?)," in *California Geographer*, 8:75–87 (1967).

Long, Stephen H. *The Northern Expeditions of Stephen H. Long: The Journals of 1817 and 1823 and Related Documents*. Ed. by Lucile M. Kane, June D. Holmquist, and Carolyn Gilman. St. Paul: MHS, 1978. 407 p. Includes "The Journal of James E. Colhoun, 1823," pp. 269–327.

Miceli, Augusto P. *The Man with the Red Umbrella: Giacomo Costantino Beltrami in America*. Baton Rouge, La.: Claitor's Pub. Div., 1974. 183 p. With bibliog.

Nichols, Roger L. and Patrick L. Halley. *Stephen Long and American Frontier Exploration.* Newark, Del.: Univ. of Delaware Press, 1980. 276 p.

Nicollet, Joseph N. *Joseph N. Nicollet on the Plains and Prairies: The Expeditions of 1838-39 with Journals, Letters, and Notes on the Dakota Indians.* Trans. and ed. by Edmund C. Bray and Martha C. Bray. St. Paul: MHS, 1976. 294 p. Includes Raymond J. DeMallie, trans. and ed., "Nicollet's Notes on the Dakota," pp. 250-281.

Parker, John. "Willard Glazier and the Mississippi Headwater Controversy," in Soc. for the History of Discoveries (Amsterdam, Neth.), *Terrae Incognitae,* 7: 53-63 (1976).

FUR TRADE

Birk, Douglas A. and Bruce M. White. "Who Wrote the 'Diary of Thomas Connor'? A Fur Trade Mystery," in *MH,* 46:170-188 (Spring, 1979), and "Guilty as Charged," attributing the diary to John Sayer on the basis of handwriting analysis, in *MH,* 47:162 (Winter, 1980).

Brehaut, Harry B. "The Red River Cart and Trails, The Fur Trade," in Historical and Scientific Soc. of Manitoba, *Transactions,* 3rd series, 28:5-35 (1971-1972).

"Fur Trade," in *Roots,* vol. 5, no. 1 (Fall, 1976). 31 p.

Gilman, Rhoda R. "The Fur Trade in the Upper Mississippi Valley, 1630-1850," in *Wisconsin Magazine of History,* 58:2-18 (Autumn, 1974).

Johns, Verlan R. and others. "An Early Nineteenth Century Occupation of Pike Island, Dakota County, Minnesota," in *Minnesota Archaeologist,* 36:50-60 (July, 1976).

Judd, Carol M. and Arthur J. Ray, eds. *Old Trails and New Directions: Papers of the Third North American Fur Trade Conference.* Toronto: Univ. of Toronto Press, 1980. 337 p. With bibliog.

Wheeler, Robert C. and others. *Voices from the Rapids: An Underwater Search for Fur Trade Artifacts, 1960-73.* (Minn. Historical Archaeology Series 3.) St. Paul: MHS, 1975. 115 p. With bibliog.

White, Bruce M., comp. *The Fur Trade in Minnesota: An Introductory Guide to Manuscript Sources.* St. Paul: MHS, 1977. 61 p.

BEGINNINGS OF WHITE SETTLEMENT
General

Hedren, Paul L. "On Duty at Fort Ridgely, Minnesota: 1853-1867," in *South Dakota History,* 7:168-192 (Spring, 1977).

Johnson, Hildegard B. *Order Upon the Land: The U.S. Rectangular Land Survey and the Upper Mississippi Country.* New York: Oxford Univ. Press, 1976. 268 p. Some emphasis on the hill country of southeastern Minn.

"Living in Minnesota Territory," in *Roots,* vol. 3, no. 1 (Fall, 1974). 31 p.

Smith, G. Hubert. "A Frontier Fort in Peacetime," in *MH,* 45:116-128 (Fall, 1976). Fort Ridgely.

Fort Snelling

Grossman, John F. *Army Uniforms at Fort Snelling, 1821-1832.* (Historic Fort Snelling Chronicles 1.) St. Paul: MHS, 1974. [6] p.

Lofstrom, Edward. "An Analysis of Temporal Change in a 19th-Century Ceramic Assemblage from Fort Snelling, Minnesota," in *Minnesota Archaeologist,* 35:16-47 (1976).

Mattson, Donald E. and Louis D. Walz. *Old Fort Snelling Instruction Book for Fife with Music of Early America.* (Minn. Historic Sites Pamphlet Series 11.) St. Paul: MHS, 1974. 112 p. With bibliog.

Nagle, Liza and Marx Swanholm. *The Buried History of the Sutler's Store.* (Historic Fort Snelling Chronicles 4.) St. Paul: MHS, 1976. [6] p. With bibliog.

Osman, Stephen E. "Army Uniforms at Fort Snelling, 1819-1865," in *Hennepin County History,* vol. 38, no. 2, pp. 3-11 (Summer, 1979).

Wiggins, David S. *Service in "Siberia": Five Surgeons at Early Fort Snelling.* (Historic Fort Snelling Chronicles 5.) St. Paul: MHS, 1977. 8 p. With bibliog.

Ziebarth, Marilyn and Alan Ominsky. *Fort Snelling: Anchor Post of the Northwest.* (Minn. Historic Sites Pamphlet Series 4.) St. Paul: MHS, 1970. Rev. ed., 1979. 35 p.

Pioneer Life

Daughters of the American Revolution, Minnesota, Old Trails and Historic Spots Committee. *Old Rail Fence Corners: The A.B.C.'s of Minnesota History. Authentic Incidents Gleaned from the Old Settlers by the Book Committee.* 2nd ed. Ed. by Lucy L. Wilder Morris. Austin: F. H. McCulloch Printing Co., 1915. 324 p. 1st ed. published 1914. Reprint ed., with an introd. by Marjorie Kreidberg and an index. St. Paul: MHS, 1976. 344 p.

[Dillman, Willard]. *A Human Life: Memories of a Pioneer.* Excelsior: Record Office, 1934. 175 p. Jacob Dillman of Clifton, Lyon County.

Hallberg, Jane. *The Story of Pierre Bottineau.* [Brooklyn Center]: Brooklyn Historical Soc., 1979. 24 p. With bibliog.

Knight, James K. *We Homesteaded.* New Brighton: Printcraft, 1975. 255 p. Itasca County.

Kohlhase, Sylvia H. *In the Shadow of the Spruce: Recollections of Homestead Days on the Black River.* [International Falls]: Voyageur Printing, 1974. 54 p.

Kreidberg, Marjorie. *Food on the Frontier: Minnesota Cooking from 1850 to 1900 with Selected Recipes.* St. Paul: MHS, 1975. 313 p.

LeVesconte, Lillie G. *Little Bird That Was Caught: The Story of the Early Years of Jane DeBow Gibbs.* [St. Paul]: Ramsey County Historical Soc., 1968. 54 p. Lake Harriet Mission.

Potter, Theodore E. *The Autobiography of Theodore Edgar Potter.* Concord, N.H.: Rumford Press, 1913. Minn., pp. 151–228. Reprinted, Ann Arbor: Historical Soc. of Michigan, 1978.

Rahm, Virginia L. "Scores of MHS Museum Items Date to American Revolution," in *MH*, 44:226–230 (Summer, 1975).

[Scott, Charles and Margaret Scott]. "1854 Migration from Maine to St. Anthony Village: Letters of Two Early Settlers Reveal Hardship, Surprise and Pleasure," in *Hennepin County History*, vol. 31, no. 4, pp. 18–22 (Fall, 1972).

Seifert, R. Gail. *Miles of Memories.* Bayport: Bayport Printing House, 1972. 138 p. Stillwater area.

POPULATION AND IMMIGRATION

See also Religion—Jews and Judaism

General

Bolin, Winifred W. "Heating up the Melting Pot: Settlement Work and Americanization in Northeast Minneapolis," in *MH*, 45:58–69 (Summer, 1976).

Holmquist, June D., ed. *They Chose Minnesota: A Survey of the State's Ethnic Groups.* St. Paul: MHS, 1981. 614 p. With bibliogs.

"The Immigrant," in *Roots*, vol. 1, no. 3 (Spring, 1973). 39 p.

Martinson, Henry R. *Village Commune Barefoot Boy.* New York: Vantage Press, 1976. 86 p. An unnamed Scandinavian village in the 1890s.

Miller, Orlando W. *The Frontier in Alaska and the Matanuska Colony.* New Haven: Yale Univ. Press, 1975. 329 p. With bibliog. Colonists drawn from cutover region of Minn., Mich., and Wis., 1935.

Rapp, Michael G. *A Preliminary Bibliography on Immigration and Ethnic Groups in Minnesota.* [St. Paul]: Minn. Project on Ethnic Am., 1972. 18 p.

British

Hodgson, Thomas C. *Pioneer Experiences of Four Manxmen and a Boy.* N.p.: Manx Soc. of Minn., 1980. 18 p. Reprinted from Franklyn Curtiss–Wedge, *History of Dakota and Goodhue Counties.* Vol. 1. Chicago: H. C. Cooper, Jr. & Co., 1910.

Macrae, Jean and others. *Scots Wha Ha'e: The Scottish Legacy to the United States and to the Duluth Area.*

Duluth: Scottish Heritage Committee, 1976. [31] p. With bibliog.

Stewart, John. *Building Up the Country on the Northwest Frontier.* Wadena: Privately published, 1967. 106 p. First published in *Wadena Pioneer Journal,* July 6–Oct. 26, 1967. Reprinted as *John Stewart, Pioneer.* N.p.: Privately published, 1980. 114 p. With genealogy.

Trescatheric, Bryn. "Furness Colony in England and Minnesota, 1872–1880," in *MH*, 47:16–25 (Spring, 1980). Wadena County.

Finns

Hoglund, A. William. "Flight from Industry: Finns and Farming in America," in *Finnish Americana*, 1:1–21 (1978). Northern Mich., Wis., and Minn., 1870s–1920s.

Karni, Michael G. and Douglas J. Ollila, Jr., eds. *For the Common Good: Finnish Immigrants and the Radical Response to Industrial America.* Superior, Wis.: Tyomies Soc., 1977. M. G. Karni, "The Founding of the Finnish Socialist Federation and the Minnesota Strike of 1907," pp. 65–86; D. J. Ollila, "The Work People's College: Immigrant Education for Adjustment and Solidarity," pp. 87–118.

———— and others, eds. *The Finnish Experience in the Western Great Lakes Region: New Perspectives.* Turku, Fin.: Institute for Migration, 1975. Matti E. Kaups, "The Finns in the Copper and Iron Ore Mines of the Western Great Lakes Region, 1864–1905: Some Preliminary Observations," pp. 55–89; Arnold Alanen, "The Development and Distribution of Finnish Consumers' Cooperatives in Michigan, Minnesota and Wisconsin, 1903–1973," pp. 103–130; Douglas Ollila, Jr., "From Socialism to Industrial Unionism (IWW): Social Factors in the Emergence of Left–Labor Radicalism among Finnish Workers on the Mesabi, 1911–19," pp. 156–171.

Kostiainen, Auvo. *The Forging of Finnish-American Communism, 1917–1924: A Study in Ethnic Radicalism.* Turku, Fin.: Univ. of Turku, 1978. 225 p. With bibliog. Minn., *passim.*

Ollila, Douglas, Jr. "Ethnic Radicalism and the 1916 Mesabi Strike," in *Range History*, vol. 3, no. 4, pp. 1–4, 10 (Dec., 1978).

Puotinen, Arthur E. *Finnish Radicals and Religion in Midwestern Mining Towns, 1865–1914.* (Scandinavians in America.) New York: Arno Press, 1979. 339 p.

Riipa, Timo. " 'Toimittaja Lähde': The Story of a Finnish Immigrant Newspaperman, Temperance Advocate, and Minister," in *Finnish Americana*, 3:30–40 (1980). New York Mills.

Ross, Carl and Velma M. Doby. *Handbook for Doing Finnish American Family History.* New York Mills:

Minn. Finnish Am. Historical Soc., 1980. 94 p. With bibliog.

Wiita, John. "John Wiita: Finnish American Radical," in *Range History*, vol. 3, no. 4, pp. 5–9 (Dec., 1978). Excerpts from unpublished autobiography.

Germans

Benjamin, Steven M. *The Minnesota-Germans: A Working Bibliography*. (Occasional Papers of the Soc. for German–Am. Studies 6.) Morgantown: West Virginia Univ., 1979. 12 p.

Downs, Lynwood G. "The Writings of Albert Wolff," in *MH*, 27:327–329 (Dec., 1946). Reprinted, Don H. Tolzmann, ed., *German–American Literature*. Metuchen, N.J.: Scarecrow Press, 1977, p. 220.

Glasrud, Clarence A., ed. *A Heritage Deferred: The German–Americans in Minnesota*. Moorhead: Concordia College, 1981. 168 p. With bibliog. A series of papers from two conferences.

Johnson, Hildegard B. "The Election of 1860 and the Germans in Minnesota," in *MH*, 28:20–36 (Mar., 1947). Reprinted in Frederick C. Luebke, ed., *Ethnic Voters and the Election of Lincoln*. Lincoln: Univ. of Nebraska Press, 1971, pp. 92–109.

Kulzer, Ramona, ed. *George Kulzer, 1831–1912*. N.p.: Privately published, 1970. 153 p. Stearns County.

Mann, Georg. "The Furor Teutonicus: Upper Mississippi Abteilung," in *Yale Review*, 60:306–320 (Winter, 1971). In St. Paul.

———. "Gambrinus and the German Americans," in *Texas Quarterly*, 19:72–80 (Summer, 1976). In St. Paul.

Quimby, Charles. "July, 1917, in New Ulm . . . German–Americans March in Protest: Don't Send Us to War against the Kaiser!" in *Preview* (Collegeville), 9: 16–18 (July, 1975).

Steinhauser, Frederic R. *New Ulm, Minnesota, Germans: Adults of German Birth Settled in New Ulm and Surrounding Areas, 1860*. [St. Paul]: Privately published, 1979. [20] p.

Tolzmann, Don H., comp. *German–Americana: A Bibliography*. Metuchen, N.J.: Scarecrow Press, 1975. "Minnesota," pp. 42–44.

Ubl, Elroy E., trans. *A Chronology of New Ulm, Minnesota: 1853–1899*. New Ulm: The Author, 1978. 132, [37] p. First published, in German, as J. H. Strasser, *Chronologie der Stadt New Ulm, Minnesota*, 1899. With photographs.

Wolkerstorfer, Sister John Christine. "Persecution in St. Paul—The Germans in World War I," in *Ramsey County History*, vol. 13, no. 1, pp. 3–13 (Fall/Winter, 1976).

Mexican Americans

Caine, T. Allen. *Social Life in a Mexican Community*. San Francisco: R and E Research Associates, 1974. 174 p. With bibliog. St. Paul's west side.

Goldner, Norman S. *The Mexican in the Northern Urban Area: A Comparison of Two Generations. A Dissertation, University of Minnesota, 1959*. San Francisco: R and E Research Associates, 1972. 121 p. With bibliog. In St. Paul.

Pierce, Lorraine E. "Mexican Americans on St. Paul's Lower West Side," in *Journal of Mexican American History*, 4:1–18 (1974).

Saucedo, Ramedo J., comp. *Mexican Americans in Minnesota: An Introduction to Historical Sources*. St. Paul: MHS, 1977. 26 p.

Stark, Greg and others. *Annotated Bibliography of Recent Research on Chicanos and Latinos in Minnesota*. Minneapolis: Center for Urban and Regional Affairs, Univ. of Minn., 1980. 56 p. With bibliog.

Norwegians

Boe, Eugene. "Norwegians on the Prairie," in Thomas C. Wheeler, ed., *The Immigrant Experience: The Anguish of Becoming American*. New York: Dial Press, 1971, pp. 51–83. Reprinted in Leonard Dinnerstein and Frederic C. Jaher, eds., *Uncertain Americans: Readings in Ethnic History*. New York: Oxford Univ. Press, 1977, pp. 181–200.

Dieseth, John. *The Life and Times of John Dieseth: Norwegian Boyhood, Immigrant, Engineer, and Road Builder*. N.p.: Privately published, [1973?]. 247 p.

Draxten, Nina. *Kristofer Janson in America*. (Authors Series 3.) Boston: Twayne for Norwegian–Am. Historical Assn., 1976. 401 p. With bibliog.

Grevstad, Mathilde Berg. "Journey of the Bergs—Covered Wagons to the Valley," in *Red River Valley Historian*, Winter, 1975–76, pp. 39, 43, 45–50.

Guttersen, Alma A. and Regina H. Christensen, eds. *Souvenir: Norse-American Women, 1825–1925*. St. Paul: Lutheran Free Church Pub. Co., 1926. Minn., *passim*.

Holand, Hjalmar R. *Norwegians in America: The Last Migration. Bits of Saga from Pioneer Life*. Trans. by Helmer M. Blegen. Sioux Falls, S. D.: Center for Western Studies, Augustana College, 1978. Minn., pp. 133–200. First published, in Norwegian, Oslo: Aschehoug, 1930.

Lovoll, Odd S., ed. *Makers of an American Immigrant Legacy: Essays in Honor of Kenneth O. Bjork*. Northfield: Norwegian–Am. Historical Assn., 1980. 223 p. With bibliog. Minn., *passim*.

Naess, Harald S., ed. *Norwegian Influence on the Upper Midwest: Proceedings of an International Conference, University of Minnesota, Duluth . . . 1975*. Duluth: Continuing Education & Extension, Univ. of

Minn., 1976. Matti Kaups, "Norwegian Immigrants and the Development of Commercial Fisheries along the North Shore of Lake Superior: 1870–1895," pp. 21–34; Carl H. Chrislock, "The Norwegian–American Impact on Minnesota Politics: How Far 'Left-of-Center'?" pp. 106–116.

Ohme, Thor. *A Few Notes from Traveling through Life.* Minneapolis: Privately published, [1975]. 68 p.

Swedes

Andersson, Per. "Per Andersson's Letters from Chisago Lake," trans. and ed. by Emeroy Johnson, in *Swedish Pioneer Historical Quarterly*, 24:3–31 (Jan., 1973).

Beijbom, Ulf. "The Historiography of Swedish America," trans. by Raymond Jarvi, in *Swedish Pioneer Historical Quarterly*, 31:257–285 (Oct., 1980).

Dowie, J. Iverne and Ernest M. Espelie, eds. *The Swedish Immigrant Community in Transition: Essays in Honor of Dr. Conrad Bergendoff.* Rock Island, Ill.: Augustana Historical Soc., 1963. 246 p. With bibliog. of Bergendoff's writings. Minn., *passim.*

Gump, Gertrude. *The Story of Swan Johan Turnblad.* Minneapolis: Am. Swedish Institute, 1969. 12 p. Editor of *Svenska Amerikanska Posten.*

Hallonquist, Einar. "I Was a Farm Hand on the Prairie in Minnesota," in *The Bridge* (Karlstad, Swed.), 8:4–7, 13, 14 (1976). Southwestern Minn.

Hasselmo, Nils. *Swedish America: An Introduction.* Minneapolis: Swedish Information Service, 1976. 70 p.

———, ed. *Perspectives on Swedish Immigration: Proceedings of the International Conference on the Swedish Heritage in the Upper Midwest . . . 1976.* Chicago: Swedish Pioneer Historical Soc., 1978. 349 p. Collection of conference papers.

Johnson, Elroy. *Jonas H.* N.p.: Privately published, 1976. [97] p. Life of Jonas H. Johnson in Becker County.

———, ed. *A Guide to Swedish Minnesota.* Minneapolis: Minn. Am. Swedish Council, 1980. 57 p.

Kastrup, Allan. *The Swedish Heritage in America: The Swedish Element in America and American–Swedish Relations in Their Historical Perspective.* [Minneapolis]: Swedish Council of Am., 1975. Minn., pp. 196–206, 334–337, 401–421.

Lindmark, Sture. *Swedish America, 1914–1932: Studies in Ethnicity with Emphasis on Illinois and Minnesota.* (Studia Historica Upsaliensia 37.) Chicago: Swedish Pioneer Historical Soc., 1971. 360 p. With bibliog.

Ljungmark, Lars. "Hans Mattson's *Minnen:* A Swedish–American Monument," in *Swedish Pioneer Historical Quarterly*, 29:57–68 (Jan., 1978).

McKnight, Roger. "Andrew Peterson's Journals: An Analysis," in *Swedish Pioneer Historical Quarterly*, 28:153–172 (July, 1977). Carver County.

———, trans. and ed. "Andrew Peterson's Emigrant Voyage of 1850," in *Swedish Pioneer Historical Quarterly*, 31:3–11 (Jan., 1980).

Minnesota American Swedish Bicentennial Council. *A Guide to Swedish Minnesota.* Minneapolis, 1973. [62] p. Swedish concentrations in the Twin Cities, Duluth area, and Washington, Chisago, Isanti, Goodhue, Carver, Nicollet, Kandiyohi, Meeker, and Douglas counties.

———. *Swedish Minnesota: A Bicentennial Salute.* St. Paul: North Central Pub. Co., 1976. [64] p.

Myhrman, Anders. "The Finland Swedes in America," in *Swedish Pioneer Historical Quarterly*, 31:16–33 (Jan., 1980).

Nordstrom, Byron J. "Evelina Månsson and the Memoir of an Urban Labor Migrant," in *Swedish Pioneer Historical Quarterly*, 31:182–195 (July, 1980).

———, ed. *The Swedes in Minnesota.* Minneapolis: T. S. Denison, 1976. 107 p. With bibliog. A project of the Minn. Am. Swedish Bicentennial Council.

Olson, Olof. "A Letter from One Generation to Another," in *Swedish Pioneer Historical Quarterly*, 24:242–258 (Oct., 1973). Isanti County.

Olsson, Nils W. "The Swedish Brothers: An Experiment in Immigrant Mutual Aid," in *Swedish Pioneer Historical Quarterly*, 25:220–229 (July–Oct., 1974). Minneapolis sick benefit society.

Ostergren, Robert C. "A Community Transplanted: The Formative Experience of a Swedish Immigrant Community in the Upper Middle West," in *Journal of Historical Geography*, 5:189–212 (Apr., 1979). Isanti County.

———. "Cultural Homogeneity and Population Stability Among Swedish Immigrants in Chisago County," in *MH*, 43:255–269 (Fall, 1973).

Rice, John G. *Patterns of Ethnicity in a Minnesota County, 1880–1905.* (Geographical Reports 4.) Umeå, Swed.: Univ. of Umeå, 1973. 98 p. With bibliog. Kandiyohi County.

Stephenson, George M. "When America was the Land of Canaan," in *MH*, 10:237–271 (Sept., 1929). Reprinted in Leonard Dinnerstein and Frederic C. Jaher, eds., *The Aliens: A History of Ethnic Minorities in America.* New York: Appleton–Century–Crofts, 1970, pp. 108–124.

Tolzmann, Don H. "Colonel Hans Mattson and Axel Lundeberg: *Minnen/Reminiscences,*" in *Swedish Pioneer Historical Quarterly*, 26:221–230 (Oct., 1975).

———. "Dr. Axel Lundeberg, Swedish American Scholar," in *Swedish Pioneer Historical Quarterly*, 24:32–48 (Jan., 1973). With bibliog. of Lundeberg's works.

Slavs

Chmielewski, Edward A. "Minneapolis' Polish–American Community, 1886–1914," in *Polish–American Studies*, 18:84–93 (1961).

———. "Polish Settlement in East Minneapolis, Minn.," in *Polish–American Studies*, 17:14–27 (1960).

Minnesota Ukrainian Bicentennial Committee. *Minnesota Ukrainians Celebrate the Bicentennial of the U.S.A.* Minneapolis, 1976? [115] p.

Blacks

Fedo, Michael W. *They Was Just Niggers*. Ontario, Cal.: Brasch and Brasch, 1979. 189 p. Duluth, 1920.

Fehrenbacher, Don E. *The Dred Scott Case: Its Significance in American Law and Politics*. New York: Oxford Univ. Press, 1978. 741 p.

Griffin, James S. *Blacks in the St. Paul Police and Fire Departments, 1885–1976*. St. Paul: E & J Inc., 1978. 73 p.

———. "Blacks in the St. Paul Police Department: An Eighty–Year Survey," in *MH*, 44:255–265 (Fall, 1975).

Hess, Jeffrey A. *Dred Scott: From Fort Snelling to Freedom*. (Historic Fort Snelling Chronicles 2.) St. Paul: MHS, 1975. [6] p. With bibliog.

Howard, Oscar C. *Oscar C. Howard, Master of Challenges: An Autobiography*. Minneapolis: T. S. Denison, 1974. 211 p. Prominent caterer at Twin Cities Arsenal during World War II.

Lewis, Earl. "Pioneers of a Different Kind [in Fargo–Moorhead]," in *Red River Valley Historian*, Winter, 1978–79, pp. 14–22.

Reinhart, Thomas E. *The Minneapolis Black Community, 1863–1926*. Collegeville: St. John's Univ., 1970. 94 p. With bibliog.

St. Paul Urban League. *A Quarter Century of Progress in the Field of Race Relations*. St. Paul, [1948?]. 14 p.

Scott, Walter R., Sr., and LeClair G. Lambert, eds. *Minnesota's Black Community*. Minneapolis: Scott Pub. Co., 1976. 216 p.

Spangler, Earl. "The Negro in Minnesota," in Historical and Scientific Soc. of Manitoba, *Papers*, 3rd series, 20: 13–26 (1963–64).

Taylor, David V. "John Quincy Adams: St. Paul Editor and Black Leader," in *MH*, 43:282–296 (Winter, 1973).

———, comp. *Blacks in Minnesota: A Preliminary Guide to Historical Sources*. St. Paul: MHS, 1976. 33 p.

Other Nationality Groups

Andrada, Belen S. *The Filipino Experience in Minnesota, 1918–1953*. N.p.: Privately published, 1977. 34 p. With bibliog.

Benoit, Virgil. "Gentilly: A French–Canadian Community in the Minnesota Red River Valley," in *MH*, 44: 278–289 (Winter, 1975).

Blesi, Wayne C. *A Brief History of the New Schwanden Swiss Community*. N.p.: Privately published, 1976. [6] p. Hennepin County.

Bowen, Ralph H., ed. and trans. *A Frontier Family in Minnesota: Letters of Theodore and Sophie Bost, 1851–1920*. Minneapolis: Univ. of Minn. Press, 1981. 391 p. First published as Charles M. Bost, ed., *Les Derniers Puritains: Pionniers D'Amérique, 1851–1920: Lettres de Théodore Bost et Sophie Bonjour*. [Paris]: Hachette, 1977. 439 p. Swiss at Chanhassen.

Community Planning Organization, St. Paul. *The Hmong in St. Paul: A Culture in Transition*. St. Paul, 1980. 30 p. With bibliog.

Doche, Viviane. *Cedars by the Mississippi: The Lebanese-Americans in the Twin-Cities*. San Francisco: R & E Research Associates, 1978. 130 p. With bibliog.

Donchenko, Adele K. "Slovene Missionaries in the Upper Midwest," in Keith P. Dyrud and others, eds., *The Other Catholics* (The Am. Catholic Tradition.) New York: Arno Press, 1978. Part 7, pp. 1–22.

Gunlaugson, Frances. "History of the Twin City Hekla Club, 1925–1975," in *Icelandic Canadian*, 33:34–37 (Autumn, 1975).

Ichioka, Yuji. "Japanese Immigrant Labor Contractors and the Northern Pacific and the Great Northern Railroad Companies, 1898–1907," in *Labor History*, 21: 325–350 (Summer, 1980).

Shellum, Duane R. *America's Human Secret Weapon*. Minneapolis: Minnisei Printers, 1977. 39 p. Japanese at Camp Savage and Fort Snelling in World War II.

FOLKLORE, FOLKSONGS, AND LANGUAGE

Allen, Harold B. *The Linguistic Atlas of the Upper Midwest*. 3 vols. Minneapolis: Univ. of Minn. Press, 1973–76.

———. "Minor Dialect Areas of the Upper Midwest," in American Dialect Soc., *Publications*, 30:3–16 (Nov., 1958).

Anderson, John Q. "Another Texas Variant of 'Cole Younger,' Ballad of a Badman," in *Western Folklore*, 31:103–115 (Apr., 1972).

Fife, Austin E. "More of 'Cole Younger'," in *Western Folklore*, 32:277–279 (Oct., 1973).

Kaplan, Anne R. "The Folk Arts Foundation of America: A History," in *Journal of the Folklore Institute*, 17: 56–75 (Jan.–Apr., 1980). A Minn.–based organization, 1944–65.

Laughead, William B. "The Birth of Paul Bunyan," in *Forest History*, 16:44–49 (Oct., 1972).

Wyman, Walker D. *Mythical Creatures of the U.S.A. and Canada: A Roundup of the Mythical Snakes and Worms, Insects, Birds, Fish, Serpents, and Mermaids, Animals and Monsters that Have Roamed the American Land.* River Falls, Wis.: Univ. of Wis.–River Falls Press, 1978. 105 p.

DESCRIPTION AND TRAVEL
Through American Eyes

Andrews, Christopher C. *Minnesota and Dacotah: In Letters Descriptive of a Tour through the North-West, in the Autumn of 1856.* Washington: Robert Farnham, 1857. 215 p. Four "editions" in 1857. Reprinted, New York: Arno Press, 1975.

Ballard, Dorothy. *Horseback Honeymoon: The Vanishing Old West of 1907 through the Eyes of Two Young Artists in Love.* New York: Two Continents Pub. Group, 1975. Minn., pp. 1–66.

Kinghorn, Norton D. "Mark Twain in the Red River Valley of the North," in *MH*, 45:321–328 (Winter, 1977).

Moore, Nathaniel F. *A Trip from New York to the Falls of St. Anthony in 1845.* Ed. by Stanley Pargellis and Ruth L. Butler. Chicago: Univ. of Chicago Press, 1946. Minn., pp. 25–37.

Swanholm, Marx and Susan Zeik. *The Tonic of Wildness: The Golden Age of the "Fashionable Tour" on the Upper Mississippi.* (Historic Fort Snelling Chronicles 3.) St. Paul: MHS, 1976. [8] p. With bibliog.

"Viator" [*Pseud.*]. "Impressions of Minnesota Territory by a Pennsylvania Visitor of 1857," introd. by Paul H. Giddens, in *MH*, 46:210–227 (Summer, 1979). Originally published in the *Venango Spectator* (Franklin, Pa.), July 15–Sept. 30, 1857.

Through European Eyes

Bjørnson, Bjørnstjerne. *Land of the Free: Bjørnstjerne Bjørnson's America Letters, 1880–1881.* Ed. and trans. by Eva L. Haugen and Einar Haugen. Northfield: Norwegian–Am. Historical Assn., 1978. Pt. 2. "The West: Bjørnson in Battle," pp. 139–245. Upper Midwest lecture tour.

Bright, Henry A. *Happy Country This America: The Travel Diary of Henry Arthur Bright.* Ed. with introd. by Anne H. Ehrenpries. Columbus: Ohio State Univ. Press, 1978. Minn. in 1852, pp. 276–292.

Lakier, Aleksandr B. *A Russian Looks at America: The Journey of Aleksandr Borisovich Lakier in 1857.* Trans. and ed. by Arnold Schrier and Joyce Story. Chicago: Univ. of Chicago Press, 1979. Minn., pp. 191–204.

Mohr, Nicolaus. *Excursion through America.* Ed. by Ray A. Billington. Trans. by La Vern J. Rippley. Chicago: Donnelley, 1973. Minn., pp. xlii–lii, 67–99, 273–283. First published in German, 1884.

Sperry, Arthur. "By Steamboat to Redwood Agency," ed. by Patricia Hampl, in *Preview* (Collegeville), 9:13–16 (Mar., 1975).

Wiśniowski, Sygurd. *Ameryka, 100 Years Old: A Globetrotter's View.* Trans., ed., and arranged by Marion M. Coleman. Cheshire, Conn.: Cherry Hill Books, 1972. "Minnesota Sketches," pp. 29–50. A Polish observer, 1874–75.

GOVERNMENT OF MINNESOTA
General

Gieske, Millard L. and Edward R. Brandt, eds. *Perspectives on Minnesota Government and Politics.* Dubuque, Iowa: Kendall–Hunt Pub. Co., 1977. 415 p.

"State Government," in *Roots*, vol. 1, no. 1 (Fall, 1972). 31 p.

White, Bruce M. and others, comps. *Minnesota Votes: Election Returns by County for Presidents, Senators, Congressmen, and Governors, 1857–1976.* St. Paul: MHS, 1977. 234 p.

State Government

Benson, Elmer A. "Politics in My Lifetime," in *MH*, 47:154–160 (Winter, 1980).

Britts, Maurice W. *Billy Williams: Minnesota's Assistant Governor.* St. Cloud: North Star Press, 1977. 198 p.

Clark, Norman H. *Mill Town: A Social History of Everett, Washington.* Seattle: Univ. of Washington Press, 1970. David M. Clough as lumber industrialist at Everett, pp. 174–224 and *passim*.

Fraser, Arvonne S. and Sue E. Holbert. "Women in the Minnesota Legislature," in Barbara Stuhler and Gretchen Kreuter, eds., *Women of Minnesota: Selected Biographical Essays.* St. Paul: MHS, 1977, pp. 247–283.

Kane, Betty. "The 1876 Legislature: A Case Study in Lively Futility," in *MH*, 45:223–240 (Summer, 1977).

Minnesota Dept. of Highways, Office of Public Information. *50th Anniversary, 1921–1971.* St. Paul, 1971. 37 p.

Minnesota Legislative Reference Library. *A Preliminary Listing of Materials on the Minnesota Legislature.* St. Paul, 1977. 11 p.

Swanholm, Marx. *Alexander Ramsey and the Politics of Survival.* (Minn. Historic Sites Pamphlet Series 13.) St. Paul: MHS, 1977. 31 p. With bibliog.

White, Helen M. *Guide to a Microfilm Edition of the Alexander Ramsey Papers and Records.* St. Paul: MHS, 1974. 78 p.

Local Government

Fahrendorff, Ruth. *The History of the Golden Valley Volunteer Fire Department: Looking Back from 1980.* Golden Valley: Historical Soc., [1980?]. 22 p.

Heath, Richard. *Mill City Firefighters: The First Hundred Years, 1879-1979.* Minneapolis: Extra Alarm Assn. of the Twin Cities, 1981. 240 p. With maps.

St. Paul, Fire and Safety Services Dept. *Proud Traditions: A History in Words and Photos of St. Paul Firefighters, 1854-1979.* St. Paul, 1979. 148 p.

Writers' Program, Minnesota. *The Mayors of St. Paul, 1850-1940, including the First Three Town Presidents.* St. Paul: [City Council?], 1940. 73 p.

Crime and the Courts
CRIME AND PUNISHMENT

Brooks, Tim. "The Last Words of Harry Hayward (A True Record Mystery)," in *Antique Phonograph Monthly*, 1:1-9 (June–July, 1973). Murder of Kitty Ging in Minneapolis.

Cantrell, Dallas. *Youngers' Fatal Blunder: Northfield, Minnesota.* San Antonio: Naylor Co., 1973. 152 p. With bibliog. Author's reconstruction of the bank robbery and capture.

Ferrell, Paul. *Michigan Mossback: From Green Pine Woods and Logging Roads to Big City Rackets.* Minneapolis: The Author, 1938. 172 p. Twin Cities. Reminiscences.

Giese, Donald J. *The Carol Thompson Murder Case.* New York: Scope Reports, 1969. 274 p.

Graham, Don. "*The Great Northfield Minnesota Raid* and the Cinematic Legend of Jesse James," in *Journal of Popular Film*, 6:77-85 (1977).

Holbrook, Stewart H. *Murder Out Yonder: An Informal Study of Certain Classic Crimes in Back-Country America.* New York: Macmillan, 1941. "Kitty Ging's Buggy Ride," pp. 69-93. Minneapolis.

Jefferson, Ted. *One Bad Dude: The Miraculous Transformation of a Four-Time Loser.* Kalamazoo, Mich.: Master's Press, 1978. 176 p. Reminiscences of Prohibition days.

Kruse, Horst H. "Myth in the Making: The James Brothers, the Bank Robbery at Northfield, Minn., and the Dime Novel," in *Journal of Popular Culture*, 10:315-325 (Fall, 1976).

McDonald, Joan. *A History of the Minnesota Home School, 1911-1976.* Sauk Centre: The School, 1976. 57 p. With bibliog. A correctional institution for juveniles in Sauk Centre.

Nienaber, Craig. "Gangsterland in the '30s: Major Criminal Activity Flourished for More than a Decade in Minneapolis Thanks to Prohibition and Corruption," in *Hennepin County History*, vol. 36, no. 4, pp. 3-9 (Winter, 1977-78); vol. 37, no. 1, pp. 15-19 (Spring, 1978).

Samaha, Joel. "A Case of Murder: Criminal Justice in Early Minnesota," in *Minnesota Law Review*, 60: 1219-1231 (June, 1976). Murder of Michael Dugan in Anoka, 1860. Emphasizes social background of judges, sheriff, and jury.

COURTS AND LAWYERS

Sheran, Robert J. and Timothy J. Baland. *The Law, Courts, and Lawyers in the Frontier Days of Minnesota: An Informal Legal History of the Years 1835 to 1865.* [St. Paul?: William Mitchell College of Law, 1976?]. 52 p. First published in *William Mitchell Law Review*, 2:1-52 (1976).

Ueland, Sigurd. *Sense and Senility: A Commonplace Biography.* Shafer: Privately published, 1971. 107 p. Autobiography.

U.S. Judicial Conference Bicentennial Committee. *A History of the United States Court of Appeals for the Eighth Circuit.* Washington: GPO, 1977. 103 p. With biographical sketches.

State Capitol

Hitchcock, Henry R. and William Seale. *Temples of Democracy: The State Capitols of the USA.* New York: Harcourt Brace Jovanovich, 1976. Minn., pp. 215-226.

Thompson, Neil B. "A Half Century of Capital Conflict: How St. Paul Kept the Seat of Government," in *MH*, 43:238-254 (Fall, 1973).

———. *Minnesota's State Capitol: The Art and Politics of a Public Building.* (Minn. Historic Sites Pamphlet Series 9.) St. Paul: MHS, 1974. 100 p.

Taxation and Public Finance

Gaylord, Kathleen A. and Susan C. Jacobson. *History of Taxation in Minnesota.* Rev. 2nd ed. St. Paul: Minn. Tax Study Commission, 1979. 93 p. 1st ed. published 1978. With bibliog.

McGrane, Reginald. *Foreign Bondholders and American State Debts.* New York: Macmillan, 1935. Minn., pp. 322-334.

POLITICS AND PARTIES
General

Fridley, Russell W. *The Right to Vote in Minnesota.* Minneapolis: Northwestern National Bank, 1976. [15] p.

Hargraves, Mildred F. *The First Fifty Years: League of Women Voters of Minnesota, 1919-1969.* St. Paul: The League, 1969. 40 p.

Hathaway, William L. *Minnesota Politics & Parties Today.* St. Paul: Carter & Locey Publications, 1978. 154 p.

Yount, Neala. "Midwestern Politics: A Woman's History," in *North Country Anvil* (Millville), Aug.–Sept., 1977, pp. 9–12. On Minn. politics.

Democratic and Republican Parties

Adams, Elmer E. *The Battles of Democracy: A History of the Struggles of the Party in Otter Tail County during the First and Second Administrations of Grover Cleveland and the Reign of 'Me and Mike.'* N.p.: Privately published, 1913. 19 p.

Johnson, Dolores De B. "Anna Dickie Olesen: Senate Candidate," in Barbara Stuhler and Gretchen Kreuter, eds., *Women of Minnesota: Selected Biographical Essays*. St. Paul: MHS, 1977, pp. 226–246.

Pahl, Thomas L. *The Minnesota Republican Neighbor-to-Neighbor Drive: Successful Small Gift Solicitation*. Princeton, N.J.: Citizens' Research Foundation, 1971. 28 p.

Farmer–Labor Party

Berman, Hyman. "Political Antisemitism in Minnesota during the Great Depression," in *Jewish Social Studies*, 38:247–264 (Summer–Fall, 1976). Leadership and policies of Farmer–Labor party.

Gieske, Millard L. *Minnesota Farmer–Laborism: The Third Party Alternative*. Minneapolis: Univ. of Minn. Press, 1979. 389 p.

Lovin, Hugh T. "The Fall of Farmer–Labor Parties, 1936–1938," in *Pacific Northwest Quarterly*, 62:16–26 (Jan., 1971).

Lundeen, Ernest. "A Partial Record of the Farmer–Labor Party since 1931," in *Congressional Record*, vol. 80, pt. 9, pp. 9694–9725 (June 17, 1936). Reprinted in Dan C. McCurry, ed. *The Farmer–Labor Party: History, Platform and Programs*. New York: Arno Press, 1975. Unpaginated.

Miller, Donald L. *The New American Radicalism: Alfred M. Bingham and Non-Marxian Insurgency in the New Deal Era*. Port Washington, N.Y.: Kennikat Press, 1979. 240 p. Farmer–Labor party and Howard Y. Williams, *passim*.

Tselos, George. "The Farmer–Labor Party in Minnesota: 1918–1944," in *International Socialist Review*, 32:14–19, 26, 27 (May, 1971).

Weinstein, James. "Radicalism in the Midst of Normalcy," in *Journal of American History*, 52:773–790 (Mar., 1966). 1919–24.

Tradition of Protest

Abrahams, Edward H. "Ignatius Donnelly and the Apocalyptic Style," in *MH*, 46:102–111 (Fall, 1978).

Axelrad, Allan M. "Ideology and Utopia in the Works of Ignatius Donnelly," in *American Studies*, 12:47–65 (Fall, 1971).

Baker, J. Wayne. "Populist Themes in the Fiction of Ignatius Donnelly," in *American Studies*, 14:65–83 (Fall, 1973).

Beecher, John. *Tomorrow is a Day: A Story of the People in Politics*. Chicago: Vanguard Books, 1980. 386 p.

Boase, Paul H., ed. *The Rhetoric of Protest and Reform, 1878–1898*. Athens: Ohio Univ. Press, 1980. Paul Crawford, "The Farmer Assesses His Role In Society," pp. 101–131. Granger movement and Ignatius Donnelly.

Duoos, Robert. "The Socialist[s] in Isanti County," in *Minnesota Genealogist*, 6:9–12 (Dec., 1975).

Gilman, Rhoda R. "Eva McDonald Valesh: Minnesota Populist," in Barbara Stuhler and Gretchen Kreuter, eds., *Women of Minnesota: Selected Biographical Essays*. St. Paul: MHS, 1977, pp. 55–76.

Goodwyn, Lawrence. *Democratic Promise: The Populist Movement in America*. New York: Oxford Univ. Press, 1976. 718 p. With bibliog. Ignatius Donnelly, *passim*.

Klepper, Robert. *The Economic Bases for Agrarian Protest Movements in the United States, 1870–1900*. New York: Arno Press, 1978. 378 p. With bibliog.

MacDougall, Curtis D. *Gideon's Army*. 3 vols. New York: Marzani & Munsell, 1965. Progressive party in Minn., 1948, 2:445–452; 3:796–797.

Nord, David P. "Minneapolis and the Pragmatic Socialism of Thomas Van Lear," in *MH*, 45:2–10 (Spring, 1976).

Periam, Jonathan. *The Groundswell: A History of the Origin, Aims, and Progress of the Farmers' Movement*. Wilmington, Del.: Scholarly Resources, 1973. 576 p. First published, Cincinnati: E. Hannaford and Co., 1874. Oliver H. Kelley.

Reinhart, Cornel J. "Populist Ideology: Mirror or Prism of the Gilded Age?" in *North Dakota Quarterly*, 43:4–15 (Summer, 1975). Ignatius Donnelly and the Minneapolis "Millers' Ring."

Youngdale, James M. *Populism: A Psychohistorical Perspective*. Port Washington, N.Y.: Kennikat Press, 1975. 220 p. With bibliog. Based on upper Midwest evidence.

MINNESOTANS IN NATIONAL AFFAIRS

Minnesotans in Congress

Anderson, David D. *Ignatius Donnelly*. Boston: Twayne Publishers, 1980. 129 p. With bibliog.

Bockelman, Wilfred. *Politics with Integrity: Al Quie of Minnesota*. Minneapolis: The Eye of the Needle, 1978. 128 p.

Larson, Bruce L. "The Early Life of Charles A. Lindbergh, Sr., 1859–1883," in *Swedish Pioneer Historical Quarterly*, 24:203–222 (Oct., 1973).

Lewis, Finlay. *Mondale: Portrait of an American Politician.* New York: Harper, 1980. 287 p. Walter F. Mondale.

Lucas, Richard B. *Charles August Lindbergh, Sr.: A Case Study of Congressional Insurgency, 1906–1912.* (Studia Historica Upsaliensia 61.) Uppsala, [Swed.]: Acta Universitatis Upsaliensis, 1974. 170 p. With bibliog.

Schlup, Leonard. "Charles A. Towne and the Vice–Presidential Question of 1900," in *North Dakota History,* 44:14–20 (Winter, 1977).

Presidential Candidates

Berman, Edgar. *Hubert: The Triumph and Tragedy of the Humphrey I Knew.* New York: G. P. Putnam's Sons, 1979. 300 p.

Chester, Lewis and others. *An American Melodrama: The Presidential Campaign of 1968.* New York: Viking Press, 1969. 814 p. With bibliog.

Cohen, Dan. *Undefeated: The Life of Hubert H. Humphrey.* Minneapolis: Lerner, 1978. 519 p.

Humphrey, Hubert H. *The Education of a Public Man: My Life and Politics.* Ed. by Norman Sherman. Garden City, N.Y.: Doubleday, 1976. 513 p.

Manfred, Frederick. "Hubert Horatio Humphrey: A Memoir," in *MH,* 46:86–101 (Fall, 1978). Reprinted as a separate.

Martin, Ralph G. *A Man for All People: A Pictorial Biography of Hubert H. Humphrey.* New York: Grosset & Dunlap, 1968. 175 p.

National Portrait Gallery, Historian's Office. *"If Elected . . . ": Unsuccessful Candidates for the Presidency, 1796–1968.* Washington: Smithsonian Institution Press, 1972. "Hubert H. Humphrey, Democrat," pp. 466–471.

North, Joseph and others. *Gus Hall: The Man and the Message.* New York: New Outlook Publishers, 1970. 63 p.

Minnesotans in the Federal Government

Douglas, William O. *The Court Years, 1939–1975: The Autobiography of William O. Douglas.* New York: Random House, 1980. 434 p. Material on Harry Blackmun, Warren Burger, Pierce Butler, Hubert H. Humphrey.

Friedman, Leon, ed. *The Justices of the United States Supreme Court: Their Lives and Major Opinions.* Vol. 5, *The Burger Court, 1969–1978.* New York: Chelsea House Pub. and R. R. Bowker, 1978. Michael Pollet, "Harry A. Blackmun," pp. 3–60; Andrew E. Norman, "Warren E. Burger," pp. 461–494.

Hadwiger, Don F. "The [Orville L.] Freeman Administration and the Poor," in *Agricultural History,* 45: 21–32 (Jan., 1971).

Hill, Larry D. "The Progressive Politician as a Diplomat: The Case of John Lind in Mexico," in *The Americas,* 27:355–372 (Apr., 1971).

Kohlmeier, Louis M., Jr. *"God Save This Honorable Court!"* New York: Scribner, 1972. Warren E. Burger, pp. 107–115 and *passim.*

McCoy, Donald R. *The National Archives: America's Ministry of Documents, 1934–1968.* Chapel Hill: Univ. of North Carolina Press, 1976. 437 p. Discusses four archivists from Minn.: Solon J. Buck, Robert H. Bahmer, Oliver W. Holmes, and Herman Kahn.

Neubeck, Deborah K. *Guide to a Microfilm Edition of the Frank B. Kellogg Papers.* St. Paul: MHS, 1978. 56 p.

Stans, Maurice H. *The Terrors of Justice: The Untold Side of Watergate.* New York: Everett House, 1978. 478 p. Stans was secretary of commerce in Richard M. Nixon's cabinet.

MINNESOTA AND MANIFEST DESTINY

Baker, Robert O. "James C. Burbank, the Man Who Used Coach and Boat to Link the Northwest to St. Paul," in *Ramsey County History,* vol. 9, no. 2, pp. 9–16 (Fall, 1972).

Hoffa, Dennis. "How St. Paul Came to Lose the 'Red River War'," in *Ramsey County History,* vol. 12, no. 1, pp. 14–18 (Spring/Summer, 1975).

Irwin, Leonard B. *Pacific Railways and Nationalism in the Canadian–American Northwest, 1845–1873.* Philadelphia: [Univ. of Pennsylvania?], 1939. 246 p. With bibliog.

Senior, Hereward. *The Fenians and Canada.* Toronto: Macmillan, 1978. 176 p. With bibliog.

Woolworth, Nancy L. "Gingras, St. Joseph and the Metis in the Northern Red River Valley, 1843–1873," in *North Dakota History,* 42:16–27 (Fall, 1975).

MINNESOTANS IN MILITARY SERVICE

Ano, Masaharu. "Loyal Linguists: Nisei of World War II Learned Japanese in Minnesota," in *MH,* 45:273–287 (Fall, 1977).

Basile, Leon, ed. "Letters of a Minnesota Volunteer: The Correspondence of James M. Woodbury," in *Lincoln Herald,* 82:387–392, 438–446 (Summer, Fall, 1980). Mower County settler in the 9th Minn. Volunteers at Fort Ridgely and in Missouri, Mississippi, and Andersonville Prison.

Carley, Kenneth. "Revolutionary War Soldier Is Buried in Minnesota," in *MH,* 44:220–222 (Summer, 1975). Stephen Taylor, in Woodlawn Cemetery, Winona.

Darling, Charles B. *Historical Sketch of the First Regiment Infantry, National Guard, State of Minnesota. Illustrated.* N.p.: Privately published, 1890. [21] p.

Douglas, Donald M. "Social Soldiers: The Winona Company and the Beginnings of the Minnesota National Guard," in *MH*, 45:130–140 (Winter, 1976).

Lindbergh, Anne Morrow. *War Within and Without.* New York: Harcourt Brace Jovanovich, 1980. 471 p. Charles A. Lindbergh, Jr., and his role in World War II.

Longacre, Edward G., ed. " 'Indeed We Did Fight': A Soldier's Letters Describe the First Minnesota Regiment Before and During the First Battle of Bull Run," in *MH*, 47:63–70 (Summer, 1980).

Minnesota Air National Guard. *The Air National Guard in Minnesota, 1921 to 1971.* St. Paul: Dept. of Military Affairs, 1970. 233 p.

Nziramasanga, Caiphas T. "Minnesota: First State to Send Troops," in *Journal of the West*, 14:42–59 (Jan., 1975). Civil War.

Pluth, Edward J. "Prisoner of War Employment in Minnesota during World War II," in *MH*, 44:290–303 (Winter, 1975).

Robinson, Charles. "Fort Pillow 'Massacre': Observations of a Minnesotan," ed. by George Bodnia, in *MH*, 43:186–190 (Spring, 1973). Civil War letter.

Roth, Russell F. "Hennepin County's Forgotten Soldiers," in *Hennepin County History*, vol. 33, no. 1, pp. 4–13, no. 2, pp. 14–21 (Winter, 1973, Spring, 1974). In the Philippines, 1899.

LOCAL HISTORY

Regions of the State

THE ARROWHEAD

Fritzen, John. *Historic Sites and Place Names of Minnesota's North Shore.* Duluth: St. Louis County Historical Soc., 1974. 35 p. With bibliog.

Litteljohn, Bruce M. *Quetico–Superior Country: Wilderness Highway to Wilderness Recreation.* Toronto: Quetico Foundation of Ontario, [1965]. 31 p. Reprinted from *Canadian Geographical Journal*, 71:40–55, 78–91 (Aug.–Sept., 1965).

Lydecker, Ryck. *The Edge of the Arrowhead.* Duluth: Minn. Marine Advisory Service, Univ. of Minn., 1976. 60 p. Minn. coastal zone, the north shore of Lake Superior.

Minnesota Arrowhead Association, Duluth. *50 Years of Service to the Vacation Travel Industry, 1924–1974.* N.p., 1974. [32] p.

Searle, R. Newell. *Saving Quetico–Superior: A Land Set Apart.* St. Paul: MHS, 1977. 275 p.

Twining, Charles E. "The Long Lost State of Superior," in *Wisconsin Magazine of History*, 61:90–111 (Winter, 1977–78). Separatism in the Superior country, including Minn.

White, J. Wesley. *Historical Sketches of the Quetico–Superior.* 13 vols. N.p.: Superior National Forest, Forest Service, U.S. Dept. of Agriculture, 1967–74. Vol. 8 is *Bibliography of Quetico–Superior History* (1969).

ST. CROIX VALLEY

Dunn, James T. *The St. Croix: Midwest Border River.* (Rivers of Am. Series.) New York: Holt, Rinehart & Winston, 1965. 309 p. With bibliog. Reprinted with new introd. and revised index, St. Paul: MHS, 1979.

George, Douglas C. *An Archaeological Survey of the Sunrise–Upper St. Croix River, Minnesota.* [St. Paul]: Minn. State Planning Agency, 1973. 60 p. With bibliog.

Swain, Harry and Cotton Mather. *St. Croix Border Country.* Prescott, Wis.: Trimbelle Press, 1968. 91 p. Geology and history along the St. Croix and Mississippi rivers.

OTHER REGIONS

Christianson, Bennett M. *From the Land of the Midnight Sun to the Fertile Prairie of Minnesota: Early Pioneers and a Century of Progress.* N.p.: Privately published, 1972. 106 p. Townships of Udolpho and Lansing, Mower County; Moscow and Newry, Freeborn County; and Westfield, Dodge County.

History of the Minnesota Valley, including the Explorers and Pioneers of Minnesota, by Rev. Edward D. Neill, and History of the Sioux Massacre, by Charles S. Bryant. Comp. by George E. Warner and Charles M. Foote. Minneapolis: North Star Pub. Co., 1882. 1016 p. Reprinted by Shakopee Bi-Centennial Committee. Evansville, Ind.: Unigraphics, 1975.

Holmes, Frank L. D. *Covered Wagon Memories.* New York: Vantage Press, 1971. 142 p. Minn. River Valley in 1896.

Mather, Cotton and Ruth Hale. *Prairie Border Country: Twin Cities to Rochester.* Prescott, Wis.: Trimbelle Press, 1980. 104 p. Tour guide with historical background for southeastern Minn.

Porter, Robert B., ed. *Northwoods Pioneers: A Collection of Twelve Actual Interviews with Pioneers Living between Northome and Deer River, Minnesota.* Center City: Privately published, 1980. 32 p.

Russell, Carol, ed. *In Our Own Back Yard: A Look at Beltrami, Cass and Itasca Counties at the Turn of the Century.* Bemidji: North Central Minn. Historical Center, 1979. 128 p. With bibliog.

Thompson, Pamela M. and others. *Iron Range Country: A Historical Travelogue of Minnesota's Iron Ranges.* Eveleth: Iron Range Resources and Rehabilitation

Board, 1979. 232 p. Covers Vermilion, Mesabi, and Cuyuna ranges.

Counties

The lack of published material precludes separate listing of 12 of Minnesota's 87 counties: Becker, Benton, Big Stone, Clearwater, Hubbard, Isanti, Lake of the Woods, Meeker, Murray, Pope, Traverse, and Wadena. Consult the index for additional material on specific counties.

AITKIN

Knox, Walter F. *Pioneer Days in Aitkin County.* Aitkin: Independent Age, 1960. 5 p.

ANOKA

Anoka County Historical Society. *The Silent Cities: A Survey of Anoka County Cemeteries, Public, Private, and Abandoned.* Anoka, 1977. 246 p.

Arends, Ruby and Lucille Elrite, comps. *Some Early Deaths and Marriages from Anoka County, Minnesota, Newspapers [1863-70].* Anoka: Anoka County Genealogical Soc., [1975?]. 17 p.

Fridley Silver Anniversary Magazine, 1949-1974. [Minneapolis?]: Sun Newspapers, 1974. 80 p.

Goodrich, Albert M. *History of Anoka County and the Towns of Champlin and Dayton in Hennepin County, Minnesota.* Minneapolis: Hennepin Pub. Co., 1905. 320 p. Reprinted, N.p.: Anoka County Bicentennial Commission, 1976. With biographical sketches.

James, Jean. *The History of Ramsey.* N.p.: Privately published, 1976. 68 p.

Lyon, Louise. *History of Bethel Township and East Bethel Village That Became the City of East Bethel, From 18[54] to 1974.* N.p.: Privately published, 1974. [20] p.

Spring Lake Park Bicentennial Community Celebration, Inc. *History of Spring Lake Park, 1976.* N.p., 1976. [76] p.

"Tracks." *Anoka in 1889.* Anoka: G. H. Goodrich & Co., [1889?]. 38 p. Reprinted, N.p.: Anoka County Historical Soc., 1976.

Thurston, Harlan. *Life in Anoka—1900.* Anoka: Anoka County Historical Soc., [197-?]. [28] p.

BELTRAMI

Blackduck Souvenir Book Committee. *Blackduck Diamond Jubilee Bicentennial Book, 1901 . . . 1976.* Blackduck: American, 1976. 69 p.

Fenske, Leo J. *Carr Lake: A Community History.* N.p.: Carr Lake Farmers Club, 1976. [34] p. With bibliog.

Iverson, Myrtle. *Buzzle Township, Pinewood, Minnesota, 1898-1976.* Pinewood: Homemakers Club, 1976. [132] p. With biographical sketches.

Kelliher Diamond Jubilee Book Committee. *Kelliher Diamond Jubilee: 75 Years, 1903-1978.* Kelliher, 1978. 82 p.

Kelliher High School. *Looking Back: A Bi-Centennial Heritage Booklet.* Kelliher, 1976. [33] p. Reminiscences.

North Country. Vol. 1–. Bemidji, 1972-73, 1975–. Published annually by Hilda R. Rachuy.

Saltnes, Mrs. Nels. *Solway: 60th Anniversary Pioneer Homecoming.* N.p.: Privately published, 1958. 47 p.

BLUE EARTH

Hughes, Thomas. *History of Blue Earth County, and Biographies of Its Leading Citizens.* Chicago: Middle West Pub. Co., [1909?]. 622 p. Reprinted, Marceline, Mo.: Walsworth Pub. Co., [1976].

Lake Crystal Area Historical Society, Inc. *Beginnings: Early History of Lake Crystal.* N.p., 1979. 22 p.

Newell, Ronald J. *Where the Winding Maple Flows: A History of Mapleton, Minnesota, and Surrounding Area.* N.p.: Mapleton Centennial Committee, 1978. 128 p. With biographical sketches.

Reuter, Kelly D. *Amboy, Minnesota: A Heritage Rooted in Rural America, 1879-1979.* N.p.: Privately published, 1979. 261 p.

Wiecking, Anna M. *As We Once Were: Stories about the Settlement and Life of Blue Earth County from 1850 to the Early 1900's.* Mankato: Privately published, 1971. 51 p. With bibliog.

BROWN

Fritsche, Louis Albert, ed. *History of Brown County Minnesota, Its People, Industries and Institutions. With Biographical Sketches of Representative Citizens and Genealogical Records of Many of the Old Families.* 2 vols. Indianapolis: B. F. Bowen & Co., 1916. Reprinted in 1 vol., Marceline, Mo.: Walsworth Pub. Co., [1976].

Golden Gate Historical Committee. *Golden Gate: A Landmark of the Past.* New Ulm: Media Graphics, 1979. [132] p. Ghost town.

Scobie, Elizabeth. *Sleepy Eye.* Madelia: The Author, 1972. 150 p.

CARLTON

Luukkonen, Arnold L. "Brave Men in Their Motor Machines—and the 1918 Forest Fire," in *Ramsey County History,* vol. 9, no. 2, pp. 3–8 (Fall, 1972). Motor Reserve Corps of the Minn. Home Guard.

O'Meara, Walter. *We Made It through The Winter: A Memoir of Northern Minnesota Boyhood.* St. Paul: MHS, 1974. 128 p. At Cloquet.

CARVER

Chaska Bicentennial Committee. *Chaska: A Minnesota River City. Vol. I: The 1800s.* Chaska, 1976. 291 p. *Vol. II: 1900–1950.* Chaska, 1980. 375 p. With bibliogs.

Norwood Centennial Committee. *Norwood Centennial, 1872–1972.* Glencoe, 1972. [127] p.

CASS

Clarke, Norman F., ed. *Logsleds to Snowmobiles: A Centennial History of Pine River, Minnesota, 1873–1973.* Pine River: Centennial Committee, 1979. 543 p. With biographical sketches.

Utley, Robert G. *A Country Editor's Philosophy: Tales of the Old Home Town.* St. Cloud: North Star Press, 1976. 178 p. Reprinted from *Cass Lake Times,* 1952–76.

CHIPPEWA

Burns, Margery. *A Diary of Milan, 1870 to 1965.* Milan: Standard Print, [1965]. 280 p.

Milan Centennial History Committee. *Milan, Big Bend, Kragero Centennial, 1879–1979, Milan, Minnesota.* [Milan], 1979. 88 p.

Montevideo Community Centennial and Fiesta. *Montevideo Historical Album and Centennial Program Book.* Montevideo, 1971. 161 p.

Moyer, L. R. and O. G. Dale, eds. *History of Chippewa and Lac qui Parle Counties Minnesota: Their People, Industries and Institutions.* Indianapolis, Ind.: B. F. Bower & Co., 1916. 2 vols. Reprinted, [Marceline, Mo.: Walsworth Pub. Co., 1980?].

Quam, Agnes. *100th Anniversary, Watson, Minnesota: Watson, MN., Centennial, 1879–1979.* Watson: Centennial Committee, 1979. [88] p.

CHISAGO

Chisago County Bicentennial Committee. *An Early Look at Chisago County.* N.p., 1976. 294 p.

Cordes, Jim. *Reflections of Amador.* North Branch: Review Corp., 1976. [66] p. Swedish township.

Norelius, Theodore A. *In the Land of Kichi Saga.* Stillwater: Croixside Press, 1973. 172 p. Swedish communities of Center City, Chisago City, and Lindstrom.

———. *Sunrise, Kost, Almelund: A History.* North Branch: Review Corp., 1975. 135 p. First published in *Chisago County Press,* 1953.

CLAY

Anderson, Gary C. "Moorhead *vs* Fargo: A Study of Economic Rivalry and Urban Development in the Red River Valley of the North," in *North Dakota Quarterly,* 42:60–77 (Autumn, 1974). In the 1870s.

A Century Together: A History of Fargo, North Dakota, and Moorhead, Minnesota. N.p.: Fargo–Moorhead Centennial Corp., 1975. 224 p.

Christensen, Oscar A. *The Man Behind the Plow: A Short History of a Clay County Pioneer.* Cross Lake: Lloyd E. Monson, 1949. 14 p. Otto A. Christensen.

Fredericks, Morris P. *Early History of Moorhead in the 1870's and 1880's.* Moorhead: Lake Agassiz Regional Library, 1976. 143 p. With bibliog.

Johnson, Glenn E. *Development of Clay County—Past to Present.* [Moorhead?]: Privately published, 1975. 17 p.

———. *Here—There—Everywhere in Clay County, Minnesota.* Hawley: Herald, 1972. 162 p.

Steinbach, Jean and Sharon Askelson. *The First 100 Years: 1880–1980, Felton, Minnesota.* Hawley: Herald, 1980. 88 p.

Western Minnesota Steamthreshers Assn. and Red River Valley Historical Society. *Clay County Family Album: A History of Rural Clay County, Minnesota.* Dallas: Taylor Pub. Co., 1976. 720 p. Mainly family histories.

COOK

Humphrey, M. J. and others, eds. *Pioneer Faces and Places, Cook County, North Shore, Lake Superior.* [Grand Marais]: Cook County Historical Soc., 1979. 63 p.

Raff, Willis H. *Pioneers in the Wilderness: Minnesota's Cook County, Grand Marais and the Gunflint in the 19th Century.* Grand Marais: Cook County Historical Soc., 1981. 402 p.

Tormondsen, Chris. *Tofte: A Collection of Facts and Tales of the North Shore Area of Lake Superior.* Minneapolis: The Author, 1968. 75 p.

COTTONWOOD

Cottonwood County Historical Society. *Centennial Souvenir: 1849 to 1949.* N.p., 1949. 32 p.

Schaefer, Vernon J. *We Ate Gooseberries: Growing Up on a Minnesota Farm during the Depression.* New York: Exposition Press, 1974. 180 p. 1930s.

CROW WING

Hansen, Arvy, ed. *Cuy-una!: A Chronicle of the Cuyuna Range.* N.p.: Cuyuna Range Bicentennial Committee, 1976. 96 p.

DAKOTA

Atchison, Floyd E. *A Hole In The Curtain.* N.p.: Privately printed, 1979. 226 p. Reminiscences of 1930s Depression and service in World War II.

Braun, Carol, ed. *Reflections of Lebanon/Apple Valley, 1855–1976.* N.p.: Privately published, [1976?]. 47 p.

Burnsville Bicentennial Heritage Committee. *Burnsville '76: A Community History.* Burnsville, 1976. 176 p. With biographical sketches.

Dakota County Historical Society. *Over the Years: Historical Facts about Dakota County.* South St. Paul, 1979. 470, 67 p. Reprints of *Dakota County: Over the Years,* the society's newsletter, 1961-78, and index.

Doffing, Lucille E. H. *Hastings-on-the-Mississippi.* Hastings: Gazette, 1976. 333 p.

———— and Robert J. Olson. *Hampton, Dakota County, Minnesota: 80 Years, 1896-1976.* Hastings: Gazette, 1976. 62 p.

Fox, Darlene. *History of Miesville, Minnesota.* N.p.: Privately published, 1976. [44] p.

Jacobsen, Hazel M. *Car Tour: Some of Historic Hastings, 1850-1973.* N.p.: Privately published, 1973. 29 p.

————. *Pringle-Jacobsen Hardware Building: 207 East 2nd Street, Hastings, Minnesota.* N.p.: Privately published, 1975. [11] p.

Kaposia Days, South Saint Paul, July 2-4, 1976. [South St. Paul?]: Privately published, 1976. Includes J. Robert Stassen, "South St. Paul—Now and Then," pp. 11-19; Lucile Gower, "Kaposia Village," pp. 20-35.

Mako, JoAnn and others. *Glimpses of the History of Lakeville, 1858-1978.* [Farmington]: Dakota County Tribune, 1978. 76 p.

Randolph History Book Committee. *A History of Randolph, Dakota County, Minnesota.* [Randolph?], 1976. 43 p.

Rosemount Centennial Committee. *Rosemount Centennial, 1867-1967, Past, Present, Future.* [Rosemount?], 1967. 85 p.

DODGE

Crouch, Charles. *Wasioja: "Rooted-Yet-Evergrowing".* Tempe, Ariz.: Catalyst Productions, 1977. 142 p. Fictionalized treatment of the town's history.

Severson, Harold. *Dodge County: 125 Years of Growth.* Mantorville: Dodge County Century and Quarter Club, 1979. 258 p.

DOUGLAS

Douglas County Historical Society. *Douglas County: Album of the Ages.* Dallas: Taylor Pub. Co., [1980?]. 616 p. Contains family histories.

Schoellkopf, Peggy and Jane C. De Lay. *And Then Came Summer: Alexandria Remembered.* N.p.: Privately published, 1978. 72 p. Summer visitors.

FARIBAULT

Elmore History Book Committee. *Elmore, Minnesota: 1863-1963.* N.p., 1963. 88 p.

Faribault County Bicentennial Commission. *Faribault County, 1855-1976: A Panorama.* Marceline, Mo.: Walsworth Pub. Co., 1977. 299 p.

History of the Delavan Community, 1856-1977. Vol. 1, *General History.* Delavan: Community Centennial Committee, 1977. 170 p.

FILLMORE

Bishop, Judson W. *History of Fillmore County, Minnesota: With an Outline of Her Resources, Advantages, and the Inducements She Offers to Those Seeking Homes in the West.* Chatfield: News, 1980. 40 p. First published, Chatfield: Holley & Brown Printers, 1858.

Ellestad, Gerhard A. *Small-Town Stuff.* N.p.: Privately published, 1976. 58 p. Lanesboro.

Erickson, John, comp. and ed. *Heritage: Peterson, Minnesota.* Peterson: Station Museum, 1976. 76 p. A pictorial history.

Hagen, Edna. *Washington Community.* N.p.: [The Author?, 1972?]. 28 p. With biographical sketches.

Haven, George A. *Chatfield, Minnesota Territory: Its Settlers, Their Environment, and Their Successors.* [Chatfield]: Privately published, 1974. 147 p.

McConnell, Dorothy, ed. *The Chatfield, Minnesota, Bicentennial Bugle.* Chatfield: News, 1977. 106 p.

Rislove, Ann and John Erickson. *The Peterson Book.* N.p.: Privately published, 1974. 54 p. Norwegian community.

FREEBORN

Curtiss-Wedge, Franklyn, ed. *History of Freeborn County, Minnesota.* Chicago: H. C. Cooper, Jr. & Co., [1911]. 883 p. Reprinted, [Marceline, Mo.: Walsworth Pub. Co., 1976]. With biographical sketches.

GOODHUE

Angell, Madeline. *Red Wing, Minnesota: Saga of a River Town.* Minneapolis: Dillon Press, 1977. [528] p.

Callister, Beulah. *Literary Guild of Kenyon, 1930-1980.* N.p.: Privately published, 1980. [18] p.

Callister, Frank. *Recollections.* [Kenyon?]: Privately published, 1978. 153 p. Rural life around Skyberg (abandoned) and Kenyon, 1910-71.

Cannon Falls Bicentennial Heritage Committee. *Chronicles of Cannon Falls.* Cannon Falls: Beacon, 1976. 163 p.

Goodhue County Historical News. Vol. 1-. Red Wing, 1967-. Published three times a year by the Goodhue County Historical Soc.

Goodhue Diamond Jubilee Committee. *Goodhue Diamond Jubilee, 1897-1972.* Goodhue: Goodhue County Tribune, 1972. 120 p.

Graham, H. E. *A Souvenir . . . Zumbrota, Minnesota.* Red Wing: Wall & Haines, [1899?]. [39] p.

Holst, Gladys V. *The Octagon House*. Red Wing: Privately published, 1974. 20 p. With bibliog.

Red Wing City Planning Staff. *Levee Park: Gateway to the City Beautiful*. [Red Wing?], 1979. [24] p.

Severson, Harold. *We Give You—Kenyon*. Kenyon: Security State Bank, 1976. 232 p. With biographical sketches. Norwegian community.

GRANT

Ashby, Minnesota: "The Town That Aspired to Be a Metropolis," 1879–1979. Battle Lake: Review, 1979. 85 p. Contains biographical sketches. Includes John A. Quist, "Ashby, 1879–1904: The Formative Years," pp. 1–38; Robert Jensen, "A Review of Ashby Town Team Baseball," pp. 38–49.

Hedstrom, Gary W. *A Blossom on the Prairie: The History of the Herman, Minnesota, Area Through 1900*. Herman: Review, 1976. 99 p.

HENNEPIN

Anderson, Helen H. *Eden Prairie: The First 100 Years*. Eden Prairie: Historical Soc. and Cultural Commission, 1979. 139 p.

Chandler, D. C. *Champlin on the Mississippi*. N.p.: Champlin Bicentennial Historical Projects, 1979. 365 p. With biographical sketches.

Deane, Jim [James]. *Maple Grove Memories*. Maple Grove: Bicentennial Steering Committee, 1977. [30] p.

Duff, Nicholas E. *Maplewood*. N.p.: Privately published, 1976. 26 p. Deals with the development of a small peninsula in Wayzata Bay, Lake Minnetonka, for tourists.

Excelsior–Lake Minnetonka Historical Society and Excelsior City Council. *The Lake, the Land, and the People: A Historical Portrait of the City of Excelsior, as Seen in Its Buildings and Sites*. Excelsior, 1978. 69 p.

Hennepin County Park Reserve District. *The First 20 Years: The Story of the Hennepin County Park Reserve District*. Maple Plain, 1977. 18 p.

Leipold, La Verna. *The Lake Minnetonka Book of Days*. Excelsior: Leipold's, 1975. [122] p. With bibliog.

Meyer, Ellen W. *Happenings Around Deephaven: The First Hundred Years, 1853–1953*. N.p.: Excelsior–Lake Minnetonka Historical Soc., 1978. 93 p.

———. *Happenings Around Wayzata: The First Hundred Years, 1853–1953*. Excelsior: Tonka Printing Co., 1980. 123 p.

Morrison, Mary H. *Highcroft, 1895–1952*. N.p.: Privately published, [1952?]. 26 p. Heffelfinger home at Wayzata.

Richards, Bergmann. *Minnetonka Beach: Our History, Our Municipality, Our Home Rule Charter, 1855–1955*. N.p.: Minnetonka Beach Civic Assn., [1955?]. 87 p.

Svendsen, Gustav R. *Hennepin County History: An Illustrated Essay*. Minneapolis: Hennepin County Historical Soc., 1976. 95 p.

Thibault, Isabel. *My Island: Memories of a Childhood on Gale's Island*. Excelsior: Excelsior-Lake Minnetonka Historical Soc., 1978. 31 p.

HOUSTON

Bissen, Barbara, comp. and ed. *Greetings from Hokah, Minnesota*. Hokah: Privately published, 1975. 55 p.

[Eitzen Bicentennial Committee?]. *Bits O' the Past of the Eitzen Community*. N.p.: Privately published, [1976?]. 20 p.

Walhovd, Carol and Fern Heiller. *The Brownsville Story*. Winona: St. Mary's College Press, 1976. 117 p.

Witt, Mason A. *Historical Notes of Interest: Houston and Area*. [Houston?]: Privately published, 1974. 55 p. First published in *Houston County News*, Mar. 23, 1972–Apr. 18, 1974.

ITASCA

Deer River Federated Woman's Club. *Deer River Yesterday and Today*. Deer River: Darrell R. Emerson, 1973. 114 p.

Keewatin Fiftieth Anniversary Book Committee. *Keewatin: From Timber to Iron in Fifty Years, 1906–1956*. [Nashwauk]: Eastern Itascan, 1956. 92 p.

Manske, Dorothy. *On the Banks of the Bigfork: The Story of the Bigfork River Valley*. Bigfork: Northwoods Press, 1976. 158 p.

Nashwauk Seventy–fifth Anniversary Book Committee. *Nashwauk 'From Timber to Taconite': The Story of Nashwauk, Minnesota*. Nashwauk: Eastern Itascan, 1978. 109 p. With biographical sketches.

Navratil, Patricia E. *Trails Through the Northwoods: A History of the Bigfork Trail*. Bigfork: Northwoods Press, 1976. 39 p. Lumbering and early resorts.

Northprint Co. *Photo History of Grand Rapids and Surrounding Communities*. Grand Rapids, 1976. [96] p.

JACKSON

[Freed, Dorothy, ed.]. *Lakefield's First 100 Years, 1879–1979*. [Lakefield?]: Centennial Booklet Committee, [1979]. [140] p.

Jackson County History. Lakefield: Jackson County Historical Soc., 1979. 432 p. With biographical sketches.

Rose, Arthur P. *An Illustrated History of Jackson County, Minnesota*. Jackson: Northern History Pub. Co., 1910. 586 p. Reprinted, N.p.: Jackson County Historical Soc., [1979?].

KANABEC

Peterson, Arthur G. *Viking and Cherokee: A Twentieth Century Saga*. DeBary, Fla.: The Author, 1980. Swedes in Mora area, pp. 5–32, 150–155.

Ziegler, Frank. *"Ken-a-big": The Story of Kanabec County: An Illustrated History of Kanabec County: Its Early Years*. Mora: B & W Printers, 1977. 225 p.

KANDIYOHI

Bergquist, J. Gordon. *Once a Boy: Boyhood in Willmar during the '20s and '30s*. N.p.: Privately published, [197–?]. [24] p.

Finnell, Arthur L. *The Extant Records of Monongalia County, Minnesota, 1858–1870*. Marshall: Finnell–Richter and Associates, 1980. 89 p. Contains census, lists of county officers, wills probated, deeds and mortgages, and marriages.

Kandiyohi County Historical Society. *A Guide to Cemeteries in Kandiyohi County*. [Willmar?], 1980. 37 p.

Thurn, Karl and Helen Thurn. *Round Robin of Kandiyohi County, Centennial Year, 1858–1958*. Raymond: Press, 1958. 254 p.

KITTSON

Kittson County Historical Society. *Our Northwest Corner: Histories of Kittson County, Minnesota*. Topeka: Josten's, 1979. 424 p. Mainly biographical sketches.

Kittson County Historical Society and Red River Valley Historical Society. *Our Northwest Corner: Histories of Kittson County, Minnesota*. Dallas: Taylor Pub. Co., 1976. 600 p. Mainly biographical sketches.

KOOCHICHING

Albrecht, Lorraine and Dolly Thomas. *Northome, Mizpah, Gemmell, Minnesota History, 1903–1977*. N.p.: Northome Bicentennial Book Committee, 1977. 204 p.

Pendergast, Hannah. "The Afraid To Stay Alone Homesteader," in *North Country*, vol. 2, no. 2, pp. 39–73 (1979).

Pendergast, Jessie. "Diary of Jessie Pendergast on Her Claim—West of Bemidji, 1897–1898," in *North Country*, vol. 2, no. 2, pp. 17–38 (1979).

Littlefork 75th. [Marceline, Mo.: Walsworth Pub. Co., 1978]. 312 p. With biographical sketches.

Von Alman, Charlotte. *Silverdale, Rauch and Bramble*. Marceline, Mo.: Walsworth Pub. Co., 1979. 180 p.

LAC QUI PARLE

Herriges, Ray P. *Fire on the Prairie: Memories of Lac Qui Parle*. Madison: Heritage Press, 1980. 349 p.

LAKE

Finland Schools Reunion Committee. *Keeping Our Heritage: Finland, Minnesota, 1895–1976*. Finland, 1976. 160 p. A Finnish community.

LE SUEUR

Cleveland Bi-Centennial Committee. *The History of Cleveland, Minnesota, 1853–1976*. St. Peter: Nelson Printing, [1976]. 31 p.

Heidelberg Athletic Assn. *An Era of Progress, 1878–1976*. Heidelberg, 1976. 112 p. With biographical sketches.

Kasota (City). *Kasota: A Historical Perspective*. Kasota, 1976. 48 p.

Le Sueur Bicentennial Book Committee. *Le Sueur: Town on the River*. Marceline, Mo.: Walsworth Pub. Co., 1977. 245 p.

Mach, Mae Z. *Remember When? A History of Kilkenny*. [Kilkenny]: Privately published, [1979]. 225 p. With bibliog.

Montgomery Bicentennial Committee. *Montgomery: From the 'Big Woods' to the 'Kolacky Capital', 1856–1976*. Montgomery, 1976. 178 p.

LINCOLN

Lincoln County Centennial History Committee. *Lincoln County, Minnesota, 1873–1973*. Lake Benton: Journal Printing Co., [1974?]. 210 p. With biographical sketches.

LYON

[Anderson, Torgny, ed.]. *The Cottonwood Community: "My Home Town," 1963 Diamond Jubilee*. [Cottonwood?: 75th Anniversary Committee], 1963. [146] p.

Rose, Arthur P. *An Illustrated History of Lyon County, Minnesota*. Marshall: Northern History Pub. Co., 1912. 616 p. With biographical sketches. Reprinted, [Marceline, Mo.: Walsworth Pub. Co., 1977].

McLEOD

Knutson, Margaret, ed. *The Hutchinson Legacy*. Hutchinson: School District 423 Community Education Dept. and Hutchinson City Council Bicentennial Committee, 1976. 51 p.

McLeod County Historical Society. *McLeod County History Book, 1978*. Dallas: Taylor Pub. Co., 1979. 684 p. With biographical sketches.

Plato Centennial Book Committee. *Plato, Minnesota, Centennial, 1878–1978*. Glencoe: Franklin Printing, 1978. 100 p.

Stewart Study Club. *Stewart Centennial, 1878–1978*. Glencoe: Kopy Kat Printing, 1978. 84 p.

MAHNOMEN

75th Anniversary, Mahnomen, Minnesota, 1905–1980. N.p.: Privately published, 1980. 104 p.

MARSHALL

Augsburg Bicentennial Committee. *History of Augsburg Township 158N Range 47W, Marshall County, Minnesota.* N.p., [1976?]. 64 p.

Dahlman, Anna. *Memories That Linger.* St. Paul: Survival Press, 1977. 113 p. Rural life near Alvarado.

Halfmann, Gladys, ed. *Our Town: Stephen, Minnesota, 1878–1978.* Stephen: Messenger, 1978. 231 p. With bibliog. and biographical sketches.

Solum, Nancy, ed. *Self Portrait of Marshall County: A History of One Minnesota County and Many People Who Made That History.* Dallas: Taylor Pub. Co., 1976. 808 p. Mainly family histories.

MARTIN

Budd, William H. *History of Martin County: A True and Complete History of the County from Its Earliest Settlement down to 1880.* Fairmont: Independent, 1897. 124 p. Reprinted as *Martin County before 1880: History by William H. Budd, 1897. Supplementary Notes by Walter Carlson, 1973.* [Trimont?]: Privately published, [1974]. 119 p.

Carlson, Walter. *"Happenings in Our Neighborhood": Cedar, Galena, Trimont, Elm Creek, Fox Lake.* 3 vols. N.p.: Trimont Progress–Ceylon Herald, 1967–70.

MILLE LACS

Nelson, Herman. *The Axe and the Plow: Stories of Mille Lacs.* Princeton: Eagle, 1974. 181 p.

MORRISON

Fisher, Harold L. *The Land Called Morrison: A History of Morrison County, With Brief Sketches of Benton, Todd and Crow Wing Counties.* Rev. 2nd ed. St. Cloud: Volkmuth Printing Co., 1976. 216 p. 1st ed. published 1972.

MOWER

Christianson, Bennett M. *From the Land of the Midnight Sun to the Fertile Prairie of Minnesota.* N.p.: Privately published, 1972. 106 p. Includes folktales.

Lyle Centennial, 1870–1970. Lyle: Centennial Committee, 1970. 44 p. With biographical sketches.

Mower County Genealogical Society. *The Mower County Genealogical Society Bicentennial Project.* Austin, 1976. 12 p.

———. *Tombstone Trails: Cemetery Records, Northeastern Mower County.* Austin, 1978. 53 p.

NICOLLET

North Mankato City Council. *The History of North Mankato: A Community Profile.* North Mankato, 1977. 140 p. With bibliog. and biographical sketches.

NOBLES

Fagerness, William and others. *Rushmore Centennial, 1878–1978.* N.p.: Privately published, 1978. 135 p. With biographical sketches.

Hudson, Lew. *From New Cloth: The Making of Worthington.* Worthington: Calvin–Knuth Unit 5, Am. Legion Auxiliary, 1976. 125 p.

NORMAN

Johnson, Lenora I. *Under Prairie Skies: The Centennial History of Ada, Minnesota, 1876–1976.* [Ada?]: Privately published, 1976. 176 p. With bibliog.

Olson, Dorothy D. and Lenora I. Johnson, eds. *In the Heart of the Red River Valley: A History of the People of Norman County, Minnesota.* Dallas: Taylor Pub. Co., 1976. 550 p. Mainly family histories.

Twin Valley Community Diamond Jubilee Committee. *The Twin Valley Community Story.* Twin Valley, [1961?]. 126 p.

OLMSTED

History of Winona and Olmsted Counties. Together with Biographical Matter, Statistics, etc. Gathered from Matter Furnished by Interviews with Old Settlers, County, Township and Other Records. Chicago: H. H. Hill & Co., 1883. 1148 p. With biographical sketches. A shorter version of the same "History of Olmsted County" is in *History of Winona, Olmsted, and Dodge Counties. Together with Biographical Matter, Statistics, etc.* Chicago: H. H. Hill & Co., 1884, pp. 617–768. Reprinted, N.p.: Olmsted County Historical Soc., [1977].

Pries, Albert. *Ancient History of Olmsted and Surrounding Counties, With Ancient Pictures Added.* Waseca: Walter's Pub. Co., [1978]. 105 p.

Raygor, Mearl [W.] *Early Days of Stewartville.* N.p.: Privately published, 1974. 124 p.

———. *The Rochester Story.* N.p.: Privately published, 1976. 215 p.

Severson, Harold. *Rochester: Mecca for Millions.* Rochester: Marquette Bank & Trust Co., 1979. 332 p.

Stewartville Bicentennial Book Committee. *The Stewartville Story, 1857–1976: Bicentennial Edition.* Lake Mills, Iowa: Graphic Pub. Co., 1976. [520] p. First published by Stewartville Centennial Book Committee, 1957.

Webb, Val. *Rochester Sketchbook.* N.p.: Privately published, 1976. 57 p.

OTTER TAIL

Bergantine, Rosanne and others. *Otter Tail County History in Brief: A Collection of Briefly Told Events and Anecdotes.* [Fergus Falls]: Otter Tail County Historical Soc., 1976. 32 p. First published as *Otter Tail County in Vignette,* [1975?].

_____. *Phelps: A Peek Into Its Past.* N.p.: Privately published, 1970. 24 p.

Broschat, Myron. *Home Fires and Battlegrounds: The Military History of Otter Tail County.* [Fergus Falls]: Otter Tail County Historical Soc., 1977. 42 p.

East Otter Tail Historical Society. *East Otter Tail County History.* Dallas: Taylor Pub. Co., 1978. 335 p. With biographical sketches.

Otter Tail Record. Vol. 1–. Fergus Falls, 1973–. Published quarterly by the Otter Tail County Historical Soc.

Parson, Ruben L. *Ever the Land: A Homestead Chronicle.* Staples: Adventure Publications, 1978. 318 p. With bibliog. Fictionalized account of a Swedish pioneer family in Clitherall Township.

[Parta, Russell O., ed.]. *New York Mills: "Seventy-five Years of Progress," 1884–1959.* New York Mills: Civic and Commerce Assn., 1959. [115] p. With biographical sketches. Finnish community.

Thompson, Jane, ed. *1872–1972: Fergus Falls, Minnesota.* Fergus Falls: [Centennial Committee?], 1972. [86] p.

Wedul, Melvin O. *Autumn in Grandma's Woods.* Winona: Privately published, 1979. 100 p. Social life and conservation efforts, 1971–79.

PENNINGTON

Croteau, Mary. *Where Two Rivers Meet: A Diamond Jubilee History of Thief River Falls.* N.p.: Privately published, 1971. 126 p.

Pennington County Historical Society. *Pioneer Tales: A History of Pennington County, Minnesota.* Dallas: Taylor Pub. Co., 1976. 568 p. Contains family histories.

PINE

Åkermark, Gudmund E. *Eld-cyklonen, or Hinckley Fire.* Trans. by William Johnson. Askov: American Pub. Co., 1976. 123 p. Originally published in Minneapolis, 1894.

Johnson, O. Bernard. *The Homesteaders: The Experiences of Early Settlers in Pine County, Minnesota.* Staples: Nordell Graphic Communications, 1973. 110 p.

Peterson, Clark C. *The Great Hinckley Fire.* Rev. 2nd ed. Smithtown, N.Y.: Exposition Press, 1980. 139 p. First published 1977. With bibliog.

Snow, Richard F. "The Hinckley Fire," in *American Heritage,* 28:90–96 (Aug., 1977).

Swenson, Grace S. *From the Ashes: The Story of the Hinckley Fire of 1894.* Stillwater: Croixside Press, 1979. 246 p.

PIPESTONE

Beckering, Sandra. *Edgerton Minnesota: A History, 1879–1979.* Edgerton: DeBoer Printing, [1979]. 120 p.

Pedersen, Geraldine A. *Jasper, Minnesota, Celebrates the Bicentennial, 1776–1976.* [Jasper: Journal, 1976?]. 120 p.

POLK

Bolstad, Kenneth and others. *Garfield: The First 100 Years, 1880–1980.* N.p.: Privately published, 1980. 48 p.

Early History of the Village of Lengby. N.p.: Privately published, 1976. [24] p.

McCulla, Dorothy and Cathy Wright, eds. *Footprints of Yesterday: Centennial 1879–1979, Crookston, Minnesota.* Crookston: Centennial Committee, 1979. 120 p. With 24 p. supplement, "Church History of Crookston."

Martin, Toby. *Erskine's First Fifty Years in Pictures.* [Erskine: Bicentennial Committee], 1976. 28 p.

Moen, Esten. *"A Story of the Old Town": Fosston, Minnesota.* 3rd ed. N.p.: Privately published, 1944. 40 p. 2nd ed. published 1944; date of 1st ed. unknown.

Olson, Roberta J. *Fertile—Hub of the "Sand Hill Valley."* Fertile: Bicentennial Committee, 1975. 111 p.

RAMSEY

Holm, Bill. *Neuman's Bar.* [White Bear Lake: Lakewood Community College, 1977?]. 40 p. Reminiscences about a 90-year-old bar in North St. Paul.

Larsen, Howard and others. *Mounds View—A History.* Mounds View: Bicentennial Commission, 1976. 116 p.

North St. Paul Bicentennial Coordinating Committee. *North St. Paul Bicentennial Celebration.* St. Paul, 1976. 40 p.

Price, Stirling R. *L'Argenteau.* [Santa Barbara, Cal.: The Author], 1977. 29 p. A house in North St. Paul.

Ruschmeyer, Gloria T. *History of Lauderdale.* N.p.: Privately published, 1974. 69 p.

St. Paul Community Planning Organization. *Northern Ramsey County: Portrait of a Community.* St. Paul, 1978. [94] p.

Vadnais Heights Bicentennial Commission. *Vadnais Heights: A History, 1845–1976.* Vadnais Heights, 1976. 81 p. With biographical sketches.

RED LAKE

Healy, Anne and Sherry Kankel, eds. *A History of Red Lake County, Minnesota.* Dallas: Taylor Pub. Co., 1976. 374 p. With biographical sketches.

REDWOOD

Gimmestad, Bernard A. *Swedes Forest Pioneers.* Lake Mills, Iowa: Privately published, 1976. 264 p. Norwegian community.

Milroy Minnesota Diamond Jubilee, 1902–1977: An Historical Anthology. Cottonwood: Milroy History Committee, 1977. 77 p.

Vesta Diamond Jubilee History Committee. *Vesta, Minnesota: "Home of Nation's First Electric Co-op," 1900–1975.* Vesta, 1975. 39 p.

Zetetic Club. *Morgan's Roots Reach 100 Years: A History of the City of Morgan.* Morgan, 1978. 93 p.

RENVILLE

Paddock, Joe, ed. *The Things We Know Best: An Oral History of Olivia, Minnesota, and Its Surrounding Countryside.* Olivia: Book 200 Inc., 1976. 251 p.

Pioneer Days in Renville County. Morton: Renville County Historical Soc., 1980. 26 p. First published in *Olivia Times*, June 12, 13, 1913.

RICE

Carlin, Lynn, ed. *Continuum: Threads in the Community Fabric of Northfield, Minnesota.* Northfield: Bicentennial Committee, 1976. 84 p. With bibliog.

Clark, George L. *History of Transportation and [Rail] Roads in Rice County.* [Faribault?]: Privately published, 1976. 34 p.

Larsen, Erling, ed. *A Waterford History, 1852–1970.* N.p.: Waterford Community Ladies Aid, 1970. 78 p.

Little Prairie, 1855–1976. Lonsdale: Bendickson Printing, 1976. 164 p. With biographical sketches.

Swanberg, Lester E., ed. *Then & Now: A History of Rice County, Faribault & Communities.* Faribault: Rice County Bi-Centennial Commission, 1976. 357 p. With biographical sketches.

Warn, Bob, ed. *Nuggets from Rice County, Southern Minnesota, History.* Northfield: Historical Soc., 1977. [64] p.

Waterford Community Ladies Aid. *Bicentennial Book of Waterford History (and Surrounding Area).* [Waterford], 1976. 76 p.

———. *Our Servicemen: Supplement to the Waterford History Book 1970.* [Waterford], 1972. 39 p. With biographical sketches.

ROCK

Rock County Historical Society. *A History of Rock County.* Luverne, 1977. 546 p. With biographical sketches.

Rose, Arthur P. *An Illustrated History of the Counties of Rock and Pipestone Minnesota.* Luverne: Northern History Pub. Co., 1911. 802 p. Reprinted, N.p.: Rock and Pipestone County Historical societies, [1980?].

ROSEAU

Grefthen, G. Arnold. *Happy Hunting Grounds.* Badger: Enterprise, 1977. 52 p. Reminiscences of Wannaska life.

———. *A Land of Howling Wolves.* 2 parts. Badger: Enterprise, 1973, 1975. 82, 76 p.

Swanson, Alvin ("Ole"). *Back Home.* N.p.: Privately published, 1972. 46 p. Warroad.

Wahlberg, Hazel H. *The North Land: A History of Roseau County.* [Roseau]: Roseau County Historical Soc., 1975. 224 p.

[——— and others]. *Pioneers! O Pioneers!: A History of Early Settlers in Roseau County, 1885–1910.* [Roseau?]: Roseau County Historical Soc. and Warroad Bicentennial Committee, [1976?]. 271 p. With biographical sketches.

———. *Remembrances of Roseau County.* [Roseau?]: Roseau County Historical Soc., n.d. 128 p. With biographical sketches.

ST. LOUIS

Aurora Diamond Jubilee Historical Souvenir Booklet, 1903–1978. N.p.: Diamond Jubilee Committee, 1978. 114 p.

Hecimovich, Steve. *A Town Is Born: A Historical and Pictorial Review of Buhl, Minnesota.* N.p.: Privately published, [1974?]. 22 p.

Kent, Kai Kelley, ed. *Among the Tamaracks.* N.p.: Privately published, n.d. 125 p. Tamarack. With family histories.

Krier, John G. and Jonelle J. Krier, comps. *North Hibbing: Reminiscences of a Ghost Town.* Hibbing: Historical Soc., 1976. 64 p.

Lager, H. E. ("Finny"). *"Happy Depression" on the Iron Range.* Virginia: Range Printing Co., 1979. 102 p. Rev. 2nd ed., 1980. 127 p. Reminiscences.

Moran, Jacqueline, comp. *Recollections: An Informal History of the Alborn Area, St. Louis County, Minnesota.* Duluth: St. Louis County Historical Soc., 1980. 52 p.

Northern Lights: A Cultural Sampler. [Ely: Memorial High School, 1978?]. 20 p. Reminiscences of Ely pioneers.

Olson, Herman T. *Crane Lake Portage.* [Tower?]: Tower–Soudan Historical Soc., 1965. 11 p.

Parkville Reunion, Parkville, Minnesota, 1980. [Parkville: Reunion Book Committee, 1980?]. [60] p.

Pixley, Edward. *Home, 1902.* [Hibbing]: Privately published, [1977]. 22 p. Bear River.

Salmi, John. *Five Lakes.* Detroit, Mich.: Harlo Press, 1968. 52 p. Kabetogama, Namakan, Crane, Rainy, and Sand Point lakes.

Somrock, John W. *A History of Incredible Ely.* Ely: Lee Brownell & Margaret Somrock, 1976. 88 p.

SCOTT

Albrecht, Harold. *This Is Our Town.* Belle Plaine: Historical Soc., 1977. 591 p. Belle Plaine. With biographical sketches.

Andersen, Gail, comp. *Jordan, Minnesota: A Newspaper Looks at a Town.* 2 vols. Jordan: Bicentennial Commission, 1975–76.

Blakeley Township Bicentennial Committee. *Blakeley Township's Walk Through History.* Blakeley, 1976. 154 p. With biographical sketches.

Coller, Julius A., II. *The Shakopee Story.* Shakopee: North Star Pictures, 1960. 772 p. Reprinted, N.p.: Shakopee Bi-Centennial Commission, [1976?]. With bibliog.

SHERBURNE

Seelhammer, Cynthia and Mary Jo Mosher, eds. *The Growth of Sherburne County, 1875–1975: As Seen through Local Newspapers.* Becker: Sherburne County Historical Soc., [1975?]. 663 p.

SIBLEY

Schueler, W. C. and others. *Historical Facts of Sibley County, Minnesota.* Henderson: Independent, 1949. 48 p.

STEARNS

Butkowski, George H. and Vincent A. Yzermans. *The Mill in the Woods.* St. Rosa: Millwood Township Historical Assn., 1973. 102 p. German Catholic community.

Dominik, John J., Jr. *Three Towns into One City: St. Cloud, Minnesota.* St. Cloud: Area Bicentennial Commission, [1978]. 180 p.

Gove, Gertrude B. *A History of St. Cloud in the Civil War, 1858–1865.* St. Cloud: Stearns County Historical Soc., 1976. 72 p.

Miller, Joseph E. *Fifth Avenue: A Path through St. Cloud's History.* St. Cloud: Stearns County Historical Soc., 1977. 24 p. With bibliog.

Smith, Glanville. *Bicentennial Briefs: Published Weekly in the Cold Spring Record from January 8, 1976, through December 16, 1976.* Cold Spring: Record, 1977. [154] p.

Vye, J. A. *A Historical Sketch of Fair Haven—1856.* St. Cloud: Daily Journal Press, 1927. 6 p.

STEELE

Severson, Harold. *Blooming Prairie Update.* Blooming Prairie: First National Bank, 1980. 336 p.

STEVENS

Busch, Edna M. *The History of Donnelly.* N.p.: Privately published, 1972. 96 p.

———. *The History of Stevens Co.* [Morris?]: Privately published, 1976. 192 p.

SWIFT

Cooney, John G., ed. *Clontarf Centennial, 1878–1978: The Community and the Parish of St. Malachy.*

Clontarf: Privately published, 1978. 40 p. With biographical sketches.

Swenson, Vernie. *"Small Kettles" or "Mrs. Lillington to Mrs. Fairfield."* Houghton, Mich.: Privately published, 1966. 228 p. Childhood years on a farm at the turn of the century.

Swift County Historical Society. *Swift County, Minnesota: A Collection of Historical Sketches and Family Histories.* Dallas: Taylor Pub. Co., 1979. 962 p.

TODD

Redmond, Patrick, comp. *Self Portrait: Eagle Bend.* Eagle Bend: Public School District 790, 1972. 94 p.

Todd County Histories, Containing Reproductions of the Original Histories of Todd County Written by: John H. Sheets, A. H. Hendrickson, O. B. DeLaurier; Other Articles of Interest. Long Prairie: Todd County Bicentennial Committee, 1976. 441 p. With biographical sketches.

WABASHA

Haines, C. J. and E. G. Dean, eds. *Lake City, Minnesota, Including Frontenac, Villa Maria and Rest Island.* Lake City: Centennial Publication Committee, 1972. 96 p. First published by H. A. Young & Co. and the Jewell Nursery, 1897.

Lake City, Minnesota, 1897–1972. Lake City: Centennial Publication Committee, 1972. 64 p.

Russell, M[orris] C. *Uncle Dudley's Odd Hours: Western Sketches; Indian Trail Echoes; Straws of Humor.* Lake City: Home Printery, 1904. 255 p. Reprinted, Upper Saddle River, N.J.: Literature House, 1970. Russell, known as "Uncle Dudley," was a humorist in the Lake City area.

Severson, Harold. *Millville Centennial, 1870–1970.* Millville: Centennial Committee, 1970. 30 p.

WASECA

Johnson, Ronald J. *Vista '76: 120 Years of a Scandinavian-American Community.* Lake Mills, Iowa: Vista Community Anniversary Assn., Inc., 1976. 379 p. With genealogies.

WASHINGTON

Birchwood Bicentennial Committee. *Birchwood: A Bicentennial Memory.* N.p.: [1976?]. 14 p.

Blood, Tom and others. *Washington County Courthouse, 1885.* [Stillwater]: The Authors, 1976. 8 p. With bibliog.

Disabled American Veterans Auxiliary, Chapter 17. *Stillwater Business Ventures, 1860–1931.* Stillwater, 1978. 47 p.

Engquist, Anna. *Scandia—Then and Now.* Stillwater: Croixside Press, 1974. 163 p. A Swedish settlement.

Haskell, Hiram A. *Joseph Haskell of Afton.* N.p.: Privately published, 1941. 21 p.

McDonough, Richard L. and others. *The Old Washington County Courthouse, 1866–1974.* N.p.: [RAPP I-94, Inc.?], 1974. 32 p.

Rosenfelt, Willard E., ed. *Washington: A History of the Minnesota County.* Stillwater: Croixside Press, 1977. 332 p. With bibliog.

Sherman, Hila. *Bayport: Three Little Towns on the St. Croix.* Hudson, Wis.: Star–Observer Pub. Co., 1976. 75 p.

Smith, Alice R. and others. *Mahtomedi Memories.* Minneapolis: Anderberg–Lund Printing Co., 1976. 78 p.

WATONWAN

Broste, Ole K. *Coming to America in 1868.* Madelia: Watonwan County Historical Soc., [197–?]. 9 p.

Haycraft, I[saac] G. *Thirty Years on a Farm in Southern Minnesota, 1865–1895.* Madelia: Watonwan County Historical Soc., [197–?]. 99 p.

WILKIN

Wilkin County Historical Society. *Wilkin County Family History Book, 1977: A History of Wilkin County, Minnesota.* Dallas: Taylor Pub. Co., 1977. 437 p.

WINONA

Glende, Vernnell. *Our Altura Heritage: History of Altura and Area.* N.p.: Privately published, 1976. 64 p.

Lewiston Centennial 1863–1963. Lewiston: Activity Group, [1963]. [112] p.

Nilles, Myron A. *A History of Wapasha's Prairie (Later Winona, Minnesota), 1660–1853.* [Winona]: Winona County Am. Bicentennial Committee, 1978. 32 p. With bibliog. A Dakota Indian village.

Voelker, Theodore. *I Grew Up in West Burns Valley.* Winona: St. Mary's College Press, 1971. 150 p.

WRIGHT

Curtiss–Wedge, Franklyn. *History of Wright County, Minnesota. Illustrated.* 2 vols. Chicago: H. C. Cooper, Jr. & Co., 1915. Reprinted, Buffalo: Wright County Historical Soc., 1977. With biographical sketches.

Delano–Franklin Bicentennial Committee. *Delano: Founded 1868, Incorporated 1876.* Delano, [1976]. [256] p. With biographical sketches.

Farnham, Daniel R. *D. R. Farnham's History of Wright County, Illustrated, 1880.* Buffalo: Wright County Historical Soc., 1976. 416 p. Originally published in the *Wright County Eagle* and the *Delano Eagle,* 1880–83. The accounts of Southside, Stockholm, Victor, and Woodland townships were never published.

Lamson, Frank B. *Cokato, Wright County, 1888–1892: Personal Recollections of Frank B. Lamson.* Cokato: Privately published, [1943]. [31] p.

Lee, Carlton R. *Cokato Centennial Scrapbook: 100 Years, 1878–1978.* Cokato: Enterprise, [1978?]. 84 p.
———. *Cokato's First Century, 1878–1978.* Cokato: Centennial Commission, 1979. 116 p.

Myers, Mouraine B. *101 Best Stories of Wright County, Minnesota.* Buffalo: KRWC (radio and television station), [1976]. 82 p.

100 Years of the Good Life, 1878–1978, Howard Lake, Minnesota. Howard Lake: Centennial Book Committee, 1978. 140 p.

Waverly Centennial, 1869–1969. [Waverly: Centennial Committee?, 1969?]. 74 p.

YELLOW MEDICINE

Canby Centennial Book Committee. *People and Their Histories: Canby, Minnesota, 1879–1979.* [Canby?, 1979?]. 296 p. Collection of family histories.

Hammer Centennial Committee. *Hammer Township Centennial, 1877–1977.* Canby: Print Shop, [1977?]. 48 p.

Narvestad, Carl and Amy Narvestad. *Granite Falls, 1879–1979: A Century's Search for Quality of Life.* Granite Falls: Centennial Committee, 1979. 168 p.

Oshkosh Centennial: "Days of Our Future Past," 1879–1979. Canby: Print Shop, [1979]. 52 p.

Yellow Medicine County Historical Society. *Yellow Medicine County Heritage.* [Granite Falls, 1976?]. 36 p.

Cities

TWIN CITIES

Abler, Ronald and others. *The Twin Cities of St. Paul and Minneapolis.* Cambridge, Mass.: Ballinger Pub. Co., [1976?]. 69 p. Also published in Assn. of Am. Geographers, Comparative Metropolitan Analysis Project, *Contemporary Metropolitan America.* Cambridge, Mass.: Ballinger Pub. Co., 1976, 3:355–423.

Common Ground. Nos. 1–7. Minneapolis, 1974–76. Published three times yearly by New Vocations Project of Crossroads Resource Center. Contains 11 Twin Cities neighborhood histories.

Ervin, Jean A. *The Twin Cities Perceived: A Study in Words and Drawings.* Minneapolis: Univ. of Minn. Press, 1976. 143 p.

Johnson, Hildegard B. *An Introduction to the Geography of the Twin Cities.* St. Paul: Macalester College, 1970. 41 p. A "modified rendition" of "Die Twin Cities am oberen Mississippi," in *Geographische Zeitschrift* (Heidelberg, Ger.), 54:269–294 (Dec., 1966).

Smith, Rebecca L. *Postwar Housing in National and Local Perspective: A Twin Cities Case Study.* Minneapolis: Center for Urban and Regional Affairs, Univ. of Minn., [1978?]. 62 p. With bibliog.

Vance, John E. *Inside the Minnesota Experiment: A Personal Recollection of Experimental Planning and Development in the Twin Cities Metropolitan Area, Including an Introduction to the Vance Papers.* Minneapolis: Center for Urban and Regional Affairs, Univ. of Minn., 1977. 117 p. With bibliog.

MINNEAPOLIS AND SUBURBS

Antenucci, Steven J. *Loring Corners: The Historic Fawkes Buildings.* Minneapolis: Loring Corners, 1980. 16 p. Located at Hennepin Ave. and Harmon Pl.

Barton–Aschman Associates [Evanston, Ill.]. *St. Anthony Falls, Nicollet Island: Landmarks at the Continent's Heart.* Minneapolis, 1961. 24 p.

Bell, Marguerite N. *The Lives and Times of Just Molly: An Autobiography.* Minneapolis: Golden Valley Press, 1980. 208 p. Family life and career in Minneapolis.

Bromley, Edward A., comp. *Minneapolis Album. A Photographic History of the Early Days in Minneapolis.* Ed. by H. C. Chapin. Minneapolis: Frank L. Thresher, 1890. [184] p. Reprinted as *Minneapolis Portrait of the Past*, with special introd. by Ervin J. Gaines. Minneapolis: Voyageur Press, 1973. [200] p.

Brooklyn Center (Village). *50 Years of Progress, 1911–1961.* Brooklyn Center, 1961. [56] p.

Cross, Marion E. *Neighbors of the Institute: A Self-Guided Walking Tour—History and Architecture.* Minneapolis: Friends of the [Minneapolis] Institute [of Arts], 1977. 28 p.

Edina History Bibliography. N.p.: Privately published, 1979. 10 p.

Flanagan, Barbara. *Minneapolis.* New York: St. Martin's Press, 1973. [176] p.

Folwell Junior High School. *Reflections.* Minneapolis: The Public Schools, 1980. [32] p. Excerpts from interviews of residents of the Powderhorn and Nokomis districts of south Minneapolis.

Frank, Melvin L. "Sawmill City Boyhood in North Minneapolis," in *MH*, 47:141–153 (Winter, 1980). Early 20th–century reminiscences.

Hall, Peter N. "Minirara, Minneapolis' Internationally Historic Falls," in *Historic Preservation*, vol. 23, no. 3, pp. 36–44 (July–Sept., 1971). Falls of St. Anthony.

Hammel, Bette J. *Minneapolis: Frontiers, Firsts & Futures: A Bicentennial Commemorative Guide to the History of the City of Minneapolis.* Minneapolis: '76 Bicentennial Commission, 1976. 44 p.

Hendricks, Judith A., ed. *Bloomington on the Minnesota: A Project of the Bloomington Bicentennial Committee.* [Minneapolis]: T. S. Denison, 1976. 157 p.

Hiscock, Jennie I. *I Remember.* Whitehall, Wis.: Dan Camp Press, [1976?]. 32 p. Childhood in Minneapolis and teaching in Sherburn, Martin County, 1881–1910.

Howe, Leone O. *Album of Brooklyn Center: A History of Brooklyn Center.* N.p.: Privately published, 1978. [91] p.

Lanegran, David A. and Ernest R. Sandeen. *The Lake District of Minneapolis: A History of the Calhoun-Isles Community.* St. Paul: Living Historical Museum, 1979. 112 p.

Larkin, Lillian M. *Won't You Come to My Tea Party?* St. Paul: North Central Pub. Co., 1979. 85 p. Reminiscences, 1870–1940.

Lowry Hill East Neighborhood Assn. *House Tour, 1979.* Minneapolis, 1979. [20] p. Contains neighborhood history.

Martin, Judith A. *Recycling the Central City: The Development of a New Town–In Town.* Minneapolis: Center for Urban and Regional Affairs, Univ. of Minn., 1978. 161 p. With bibliog. Cedar–Riverside neighborhood.

Minneapolis Board of Court House and City Hall Commissioners. *A History of the Municipal Building of the City of Minneapolis & the County of Hennepin, Minnesota: A Final Report . . . 1887–1909.* Minneapolis, 1909. 69 p.

Minneapolis Centennial Committee. *Minneapolis, City of Opportunity: One Hundred Years of Progress in the Aquatennial City.* Minneapolis: T. S. Denison, 1956. 231 p.

Minneapolis Heritage Preservation Commission. *Washburn–Fair Oaks: A Study for Preservation.* Minneapolis, 1976. 107 p.

Minneapolis Housing and Redevelopment Authority. *Major Milestones, History and Highlights.* [Minneapolis, 1973]. 20, [8] p.

Northeast: A History. Bloomington: Sun Newspapers, 1976. 48 p.

Orr–Schelen–Mayeron and Associates, Inc., and the Hodne/Stageberg Partners, Inc. *Bassett Creek Reclaimed: A Design Concept for Minneapolis.* Minneapolis, 1976. [61] p.

Poseley, Judy. *The Park: A History of the City of St. Louis Park.* St. Louis Park: Bicentennial Commission and Rotary Club, 1976. 56 p.

Powderhorn Activities Council. *Powderhorn Park.* [Minneapolis?], 1976. 15 p.

Rosheim, David L. *The Other Minneapolis, or, The Rise and Fall of the Gateway, the Old Minneapolis Skid Row.* Maquoketa, Iowa: Andromeda Press, 1978. 237 p. With bibliog.

Setter, Leach & Lindstrom, Inc. *Survey: Historic Buildings of Edina, Minnesota, for the Edina Heritage Preservation Board.* Minneapolis, 1979. 91 p.

Thevenin, Tine. *Lake Harriet until 1925*. Minneapolis: Privately published, 1979. 32 p.

Walker, Charles R. *American City: A Rank-and-File History*. New York: Farrar & Rinehart, 1937. 278 p. Reprinted, New York: Arno Press, 1971. With bibliog. Labor history of Minneapolis.

Wandersee, Dorothy E. *Historic Houses of Golden Valley: The House That Bies Built*. Golden Valley: Historical Soc., 1980. 17 p.

———. *Historic Houses of Golden Valley: The Moser House*. Golden Valley: Historical Soc., 1979. 14 p.

Wolniewicz, Richard. *Ethnic Persistence in Northeast Minneapolis: Maps and Commentary*. (Research Study 1.) Minneapolis: Minn. Project on Ethnic Am., 1973. 10 p.

ST. PAUL

Baker, Robert O. "Oakland Cemetery: 'A Safe and Permanent Resting Place'," in *Ramsey County History*, vol. 16, no. 1, pp. 3–22 ([Spring], 1980).

Benson, James K. "Social Structure and Ethnic Conflict in Frontier Towns: The Case of St. Paul, Minnesota," in *Great Lakes Review*, 4:10–25 (Summer, 1977).

Bromley, Edward A. *A Photographic History of the Early Days in St. Paul: A Collection of Views Illustrative of the City's Growth from the Earliest Settlement down to 1880*. Pt. 1. [St. Paul?]: Privately published, 1901. 22 p. Only this part published; covers 1857.

Central High History Project. *Ahead of Her Time: A Woman's History of Central*. St. Paul, [1975]. [24] p. Contains biographical sketches of women graduates.

———. *From High Top Collars to Blue Jeans: A Men's History of Central High*. St. Paul, 1976. 28 p. Contains biographical sketches of male graduates.

Empson, Donald. *Portrait of a Neighborhood*. St. Paul: Identified Treatment Area Committee, 1980. 68 p. Brief history and walking tour of standing structures in West 7th St. area.

———. *The History of the Mississippi River Boulevard in St. Paul*. St. Paul: Mississippi River Boulevard Assn., 1975. 30 p.

———. "Highland–Groveland–Macalester Park: The Old Reserve Township," in *Ramsey County History*, vol. 10, no. 2, pp. 13–19 (Fall, 1973).

———. *The Street Where You Live: A Guide to the Street Names of St. Paul*. St. Paul: Witsend Press, 1975. 181 p.

Hayes, Gordon. "Minnesota's Wandering State Fair and How It Settled in St. Paul," in *Ramsey County History*, vol. 11, no. 1, pp. 12–17 (Spring, 1974).

Kain, Sister Joan. *Rocky Roots: Three Geology Walking Tours of Downtown St. Paul*. St. Paul: Ramsey County Historical Soc., 1978. 32 p.

Kennon, Peggy K. and Robert B. Drake. *Discover St. Paul: A Short History of Seven St. Paul Neighborhoods*. St. Paul: Ramsey County Historical Soc., 1979. 50 p.

Kunz, Virginia B. *St. Paul: Saga of an American City*. Woodland Hills, Cal.: Windsor Publications, 1977. 254 p.

Maher, Michael. "Letters to Fannie Higgins: The Courtship of Patrick O'Brien," and "The Liberated Woman Patrick O'Brien Married," in *Ramsey County History*, vol. 14, no. 2, pp. 3–15 (1979).

Matters, Elberta R., comp. and ed. *Grand Avenue Promenade: History and Pictures of Grand Avenue, St. Paul, Minnesota*. St. Paul: Emporium Press, 1977. [23] p.

Matteson, Robert E. *A Search for Adventure: Part 1, The Early Years, 1914–1940*. Hayward, Wis.: Country Print Shop, 1979. 116 p.

Mechanic Arts High School. *Central Park Chronicle*. St. Paul, 1974. 44 p. Essays on city life, past and present, by Mechanic Arts students, many of them Black.

Mounds Park Junior High School. *Moundsiders, 1980*. St. Paul: Harding High School, 1980. [31] p. Interviews of Mounds Park residents.

Old Town Restorations. *Building the Future from Our Past: A Report on the Saint Paul Historic Hill District Planning Program*. St. Paul, 1975. 136 p.

———. *Selby Avenue, Status of the Street*. St. Paul, 1978. 49 p.

Rea, George A. "A Grandson Describes: The O'Briens' House on George Street [in St. Paul]," in *Ramsey County History*, vol. 14, no. 2, pp. 16–19 (1979).

Richter, Bonnie, ed. *Saint Paul Omnibus: Images of the Changing City*. St. Paul: Old Town Restorations, 1979. 144 p.

St. Paul City Planning Board. *Building Trends in Saint Paul, 1940–1966*. (City–Wide Revitalization Program Technical Study 7.) St. Paul, 1967. 73 p.

———. *Progress of Renewal in Saint Paul—1945–1967*. (City–Wide Revitalization Program Technical Study 6.) St. Paul, 1968. 94 p.

St. Paul Public Relations Coordinating Committee. *Saint Paul*. St. Paul, [1968?]. 18 p. Reproductions of several 1967 newspaper and magazine stories on the rejuvenation of downtown.

Saint Paul Winter Carnival Souvenir Booklet—1886–1961: 75th Anniversary. St. Paul: First National Bank, 1961. [16] p.

Sandeen, Ernest R. and others. *St. Paul's Historic Summit Avenue*. St. Paul: Living Historical Museum, 1978. 110 p.

Sonnen, John. "[John L.] Merriam's Vision: Rural Village between Cities," in *Ramsey County History*, vol. 8, no. 2, pp. 10–14 (Fall, 1971). Merriam Park.

Steinhauser, Frederic R. *Community Study: St. Anthony Park, St. Paul, Minnesota.* St. Paul: St. Anthony Park Assn., 1969. [198] p.

Trimble, Steven and others. *Community Cooking: An Uncommon History of Summit-University.* St. Paul: Community Cooking, 1975. 188 p. A mixture of recipes and history.

DULUTH

Lydecker, Ryck and Lawrence J. Sommer, eds. *Duluth Sketches of the Past: A Bicentennial Collection.* (Duluth's Legacy, a Special Bicentennial Volume.) Duluth: Am. Revolution Bicentennial Commission, 1976. 295 p.

A Mile From . . . MacArthur, Washburn, Chester Park, Congdon Park, Irving, Jefferson, Lester Park, Nettleton, Park Point. Duluth: Independent School District #709, 1980. 183 p., appendixes.

Minnesota Historical Society. *Duluth-Superior Harbor Cultural Resources Study.* St. Paul, 1976. 151 p. With bibliog. History of the harbor and its trade.

Musicant, Ivan, ed. "The Minnesota Seaport," in *Roots,* vol. 6, no. 1 (Fall, 1977). 39 p.

Spalding, William W. "Early Days in Duluth," in Michigan Pioneer and Historical Soc., *Historical Collections,* 29:677–697 (1901).

Tapp, Hambleton. "James Proctor Knott and the Duluth Speech," in Kentucky Historical Society, *Register,* 70: 77–93 (Apr., 1972).

Young, Frank A. *Duluth's Ship Canal and Aerial Bridge: How They Came To Be.* Duluth: Stewart-Taylor Co., 1977. 11 p.

EDUCATION
General

Bolin, Winifred D. W. "Harriet E. Bishop: Moralist and Reformer," in Barbara Stuhler and Gretchen Kreuter, eds., *Women of Minnesota: Selected Biographical Essays.* St. Paul: MHS, 1977, pp. 7–19.

"Education in Minnesota," in *Roots,* vol. 2, no. 1 (Fall, 1973). 31 p.

Jenson, Carol. "The Larson Sisters: Three Careers in Contrast," in Barbara Stuhler and Gretchen Kreuter, eds., *Women of Minnesota: Selected Biographical Essays.* St. Paul: MHS, 1977, pp. 301–324. Agnes, Henrietta, and Nora Larson.

Smith, Susan M. "Ada Comstock Notestein: Educator," in Barbara Stuhler and Gretchen Kreuter, eds., *Women of Minnesota: Selected Biographical Essays.* St. Paul: MHS, 1977, pp. 208–225.

Public Schools

Alango School Reunion Committee. *50–Year Alango All–School Reunion, 1927–1977: July 2–3, 1977.* N.p., 1977. 56 p. With biographical sketches. Angora, St. Louis County.

Alumni Get Together, 1922–1972: 50th Year Reunion, Storden High School, Storden, Minnesota. Storden: Times Print, 1972. 34 p. Cottonwood County.

Aurora–Hoyt Lakes All Class Reunion Souvenir Booklet, 1909–1975. N.p.: Privately published, 1975. 104 p. Contains sketch of each graduating class. St. Louis County.

Centerville School. *Centerville School, 1976.* N.p.: [1976?]. 34 p. The early French–Canadian settlement in Anoka County and the school system.

Harris, Lewis E. and Rae Harris. *Bootstraps: A Chronicle of a Real Community School.* Cable, Wis.: Harris Publications, 1980. 199 p. Floodwood, St. Louis County.

Inver Grove Elementary School. *Inver Grove Elementary, 1854–1976.* N.p., 1976. 28 p. Dakota County.

Minnesota Braille and Sight Saving School, Centennial Committees. *Minnesota Braille and Sight Saving School, Faribault, Minnesota, 1866–1966.* Faribault, 1966. 57 p.

Olson, Alice. *From Woodstoves to Astronauts: An Autobiography.* Stillwater: Croixside Press, 1977. 283 p. Teaching in Ramsey County.

Smith, James L. *History of the Minnesota School for the Deaf.* Faribault: The School, 1893. 83 p.

Trask, Helen L. and Jeanne H. Ward. *The History of Lake Park School, Jackfish Bay, Koochiching County, Minnesota, 1920–1926.* Ranier: Rainy Lake Women's Club, [1976]. 47 p. With biographical sketches.

Warner, Holger O. *District 33: A Complete History of Chisago County School District No. 33, Fish Lake Township, Minnesota, from 1874 to 1976.* North Branch: Review Corp., 1976. 72 p.

Private and Parochial Schools

St. Joseph's School Booklet Committee. *History of St. Joseph's School, Rosen, Minnesota, 1927–1977.* N.p., 1977. 39 p. Lac qui Parle County.

Johnson, Emeroy. "Swedish Elementary Schools in Minnesota Lutheran Congregations," in *Swedish Pioneer Historical Quarterly,* 30:172–182 (July, 1979).

Narveson, Bert H. *Luther Academy Memorial History, 1888–1928.* Northfield: St. Olaf College Press, 1951. 288 p. With bibliog. Norwegian Lutheran school, Albert Lea.

St. Francis Xavier School. *Dedication, St. Francis Xavier School, August 28, 1953.* Benson: Swift County Monitor–News, 1953. [52] p. Swift County.

Sherman, Benjamin M. *The Blake School, 1907–1974: A Chronological History.* Minneapolis: Colwell Press, 1975. 256 p. Minneapolis, Hopkins, and Wayzata.

University of Minnesota

Beck, Robert H. *Beyond Pedagogy: A History of the University of Minnesota College of Education.* St. Paul: North Central Pub. Co., 1980. 297 p.

Flanagan, John T. "A Specialist Before My Time," in *MH*, 46:17–23 (Spring, 1978).

Johnson, Sherman E. *From the St. Croix to the Potomac—Reflections of a Bureaucrat.* Bozeman: Big Sky Books, Montana State Univ., 1974. Minn., pp. 19–68.

Miller, Ralph E. *The History of the School of Agriculture, 1851–1960.* [St. Paul: The School], 1979. 171 p.

Rivers, Elizabeth A. and Margaret Jacobsen. *One Hundred Years of Growing: The Development of the Extension Home Program in Minnesota, 1858–1958.* St. Paul: Agricultural Extension Service, Univ. of Minn., 1958. 14 p. With bibliog.

Schofield, Geraldine B. and Susan M. Smith. "Maria Louise Sanford: Minnesota's Heroine," in Barbara Stuhler and Gretchen Kreuter, eds., *Women of Minnesota: Selected Biographical Essays.* St. Paul: MHS, 1977, pp. 77–93.

Sevareid, Eric. *Not So Wild a Dream.* New York: Knopf, 1946. Journalism and the Univ. of Minn. in the 1930s, pp. 28–34, 48–73. Reprinted, New York: Athenaeum, 1976.

Stein, Robert A. *In Pursuit of Excellence: A History of the University of Minnesota Law School.* St. Paul: Mason Pub. Co., 1980. 543 p. First published in *Minnesota Law Review*, 62:485–514, 857–885, 1161–1201; 63:299–334, 809–905, 1101–1219 (Apr., 1978–July, 1979).

Colleges and Seminaries

Bethel Seminary Journal, vol. 19, no. 3 (Spring, 1970–71). "Special Issue" devoted to "Outline of a Century and Sketches of the Deans." Swedish Baptist.

College of Saint Teresa. *The President's Report: Seventeen Years, 1952–1969.* [Winona?, 1969?]. [28] p.

Giddens, Paul H. *Recollections of A. G. Bush and His Associations with Hamline University.* St. Paul: Hamline Univ., 1975. 32 p.

Hamre, James S. "Georg Sverdrup and the Augsburg Plan of Education," in *Norwegian–American Studies*, 26:160–183 (1974).

Jarchow, Merrill E. *Donald J. Cowling: Educator, Idealist, Humanitarian.* Northfield: Carleton College, 1974. 485 p.

Johnson, David W. *Hamline University: A History.* St. Paul: North Central Pub. Co., 1980. 304 p.

Kennelly, Sister Karen. "The Dynamic Sister Antonia [McHugh] and the College of St. Catherine," in *Ramsey County History*, vol. 14, no. 2, pp. 3–18 (Fall/Winter, 1978).

———. "Mary Molloy: Women's College Founder," in Barbara Stuhler and Gretchen Kreuter, eds., *Women of Minnesota: Selected Biographical Essays.* St. Paul: MHS, 1977, pp. 116–135. College of St. Teresa.

Kley, Roland G. *The First Ten Years: A Report on United Theological Seminary of the Twin Cities, New Brighton, Minnesota (1960–1970).* [New Brighton: The Seminary?], 1971. 139 p. United Church of Christ.

Quanbeck, Warren A. and others, eds. *Striving for Ministry: Centennial Essays Interpreting the Heritage of Luther Theological Seminary.* Minneapolis: Augsburg Pub. House, 1977. 200 p. Norwegian tradition.

Shaw, Joseph M. *History of St. Olaf College, 1874–1974.* Northfield: St. Olaf College Press, 1974. 694 p.

Swanson, Edward. "Macalester and Its First Forty Years," in *Ramsey County History*, vol. 11, no. 1, pp. 3–11 (Spring, 1974).

Libraries

Engebretson, Betty L. "Books for Pioneers: The Minneapolis Athenaeum," in *MH*, 35:222–232 (Mar., 1957). Reprinted in *Hennepin County History*, vol. 37, no. 4, pp. 3–12 (Winter, 1978–79); vol. 38, no. 1, pp. 19–23 (Spring, 1979).

Freestone, Rob. "Minneapolis Public Library and T. B. Walker: The Politics of Library Location, 1918–1923," in *Hennepin County History*, vol. 37, no. 2, pp. 4–13, no. 3, pp. 10–16 (Summer, Fall, 1978).

———. "Minneapolis Public Library from 1885," in *Hennepin County History*, vol. 38, no. 2, pp. 13–22 (Summer, 1979); vol. 39, no. 1, pp. 3–9, no. 4, pp. 12–19 (Spring, 1980, Winter, 1980–81); vol. 40, no. 3, pp. 10–19 (Fall, 1981).

Nelson, Eva. *History of the St. Cloud Public Library, or How a Good Book on the Frontier Grew into the Great River Regional Library.* St. Cloud: Friends of the Library, 1976. 48 p.

Rohde, Nancy F. "Gratia Alta Countryman: Librarian and Reformer," in Barbara Stuhler and Gretchen Kreuter, eds., *Women of Minnesota: Selected Biographical Essays.* St. Paul: MHS, 1977, pp. 173–189. Minneapolis.

RELIGION

See also Indians—Missions and Missionaries

Miscellaneous

Benton County Historical Society, comp. *The Churches of Benton County: A Short History and Genealogical Reference Guide.* Sauk Rapids, [1980?]. 19 p.

Brainerd Centennial Church Committee. *The Word: A Century with Our Churches, Brainerd, Minnesota, 1871-1971.* Brainerd, 1971. 52 p.

Grivna, Walter. *90th Anniversary Booklet of the St. Mary's Russian Orthodox Greek Catholic Church: Minneapolis, Minnesota, 1887-1977.* N.p.: The Church, 1977. 56 p.

Historical Anniversary Album: A Survey of the Romanian Orthodox Episcopate of America and Its Parishes in the United States and Canada. Jackson, Mich.: Romanian Orthodox Episcopate of Am., 1979. St. Paul, pp. 70, 71.

Hoffa, Dennis. "The Not-So-Peaceable Kingdom: Religion in Early St. Paul," in *Ramsey County History*, vol. 13, no. 1, pp. 19-22 (Spring/Summer, 1977).

Saint George Greek Orthodox Church Consecration Album. N.p.: The Church, 1975. [78] p. St. Paul.

25th Anniversary, Saints Anargyroi Greek Orthodox Church, Rochester, Minnesota, November 4, 1979. N.p.: The Church, 1979. [56] p.

Wolniewicz, Richard. "In Whose Image? Church Symbols and World Views," in *Journal of Popular Culture*, 11:877-894 (Spring, 1978). Based largely on Minn. churches.

Jews and Judaism

Danenbaum, Ruby. "A History of the Jews of Minneapolis," in *Reform Advocate* (Chicago), Nov. 16, 1907, pp. 5-39.

Dashefsky, Arnold and Howard M. Shapiro. *Ethnic Identification among American Jews: Socialization and Social Structure.* Lexington, Mass.: Lexington Books, 1974. "The Jewish Community of Saint Paul: Historical and Contemporary Patterns," pp. 11-31.

————. *The Jewish Community of Saint Paul.* St. Paul: United Jewish Fund and Council, 1971. 46 p.

Erickson, Judith B. and Mitchel J. Lazarus. *The Jewish Community of Greater Minneapolis, 1971-1972: A Population Study.* Minneapolis: Federation for Jewish Service, 1973. [325] p.

Frankel, H. D. "The Jews of St. Paul," in *Reform Advocate* (Chicago), Nov. 16, 1907, pp. 41-53.

Lewin, Rhoda G. "Stereotype and Reality in the Jewish Immigrant Experience in Minneapolis," in *MH*, 46: 258-273 (Fall, 1979).

Minda, Albert G. *The Story of Temple Israel, Minneapolis, Minnesota: A Personal Account.* Minneapolis: Ad Art Advertising Co. and Lund Press, 1971. 138 p.

Pierce, Lorraine E. "The Jewish Settlement on St. Paul's Lower West Side," in *American Jewish Archives*, 28: 143-161 (Nov., 1976).

Rapp, Michael G. "Samuel N. Deinard and the Unification of Jews in Minneapolis," in *MH*, 43:213-221 (Summer, 1973).

Robison, Sophia M., ed. *Jewish Population Studies.* (Jewish Social Studies Publications 3.) New York: Conference on Jewish Relations, 1943. "The Jewish Population of Minneapolis, 1936," pp. 152-159.

Singer–Miller, Lael. *Rachael.* N.p.: Privately published, 1980. 74 p. A Duluth family.

Stuhler, Barbara. "Fanny Brin: Woman of Peace," in Barbara Stuhler and Gretchen Kreuter, eds., *Women of Minnesota: Selected Biographical Essays.* St. Paul: MHS, 1977, pp. 284-300.

Catholic Church
GENERAL

Lydon, P. J. *History of the Diocese of Duluth.* Duluth: Greer Printing Co., 1914. 95 p.

Yzermans, Vincent A. *With Courage and Hope: The Catholic Aid Association, 1878-1978.* St. Paul: North Central Pub. Co., 1978. 84 p.

RELIGIOUS CONGREGATIONS AND ORDERS

Ahles, Sister Mary Assumpta. *In the Shadow of His Wings: A History of the Franciscan Sisters.* St. Paul: North Central Pub. Co., 1977. 555 p. Little Falls.

Barry, Colman J. *Worship and Work: St. John's Abbey and University, 1856-1980.* Collegeville: Liturgical Press, 1980. 526 p. Reprint of 1956 edition with added epilogue.

Cantwell, Sister Laurent. *A Design for Living: A History of the Sisters of St. Joseph of Carondelet in the Northwest.* St. Paul: North Central Pub. Co., 1973. 52 p.

Lynch, Sister Claire. *The Leaven.* St. Paul: St. Paul's Priory, 1980. 71 p. Benedictine Sisters at Shakopee and St. Joseph.

————. "The Shakopee Story: Episodes of Oppression," in *Benedictines*, 31:6-15, 35-37, 58-63 (Spring–Summer, 1976).

————. *The Story of St. Gertrude's Convent, Shakopee, Minnesota (1862-1880).* N.p.: Privately published, 1977. 28 p.

Meagher, Sister Luanne. *Beginning Anew: St. Paul's Priory, 1948-1973.* St. Paul: North Central Pub. Co., 1973. 12 p. Benedictine priory in St. Paul and Maplewood.

Poor Clare Monastery. *The Light of Saint Clare: Golden Jubilee, Poor Clare Monastery, Sauk Rapids, Minnesota.* Sauk Rapids, 1974. 50 p.

INDIVIDUAL PARISHES

Albrecht, Harold. *Across the Years: The History of Sts. Peter & Paul Parish, Belle Plaine, Minnesota.* Hollywood, Calif.: J. Frank & Son, 1970. [71] p. Scott County.

Bauer, John T. *A History of St. Peter's Church, Mendota, Minnesota.* N.p.: Privately published, 1974. 12 p. Dakota County.

Berg, Richard. *The History of St. Michael's Parish, St. Paul, Minnesota, 1866-1966: The Golden Jubilee of Ordination, Father John O'Neill, 1916-1966.* N.p.: [The Church?], 1966. 29 p.

Berg, Rose E. and Beverly F. Jeanson. *St. Michael's Catholic Church, Pine Island, Minnesota, 1878-1978.* Pine Island: Privately published, 1978. 312 p. With bibliog. Goodhue County.

Berger, John G. *A History of St. Bredan's Parish, the Village of Green Isle and Minnesota's First Irish Settlement.* N.p.: Privately printed, 1968. 139 p. With bibliog. Sibley County.

Brinkman, Marilyn and Marcelline Schleper. *St. Catherine's Catholic Church, Farming, Minnesota . . . With Faith in God and Devotion to Fellowship.* Albany: The Church, 1979. 172 p. German, Stearns County.

Brunner, John H. *A Short History of St. Andrew's Parish at Fairfax, Minnesota.* Fairfax: Standard Print, 1960. 64 p. German, Renville County.

Church of St. Joseph, Plymouth. *100 Years of Living Stones: A Church Called to Greatness.* N.p., [1977]. [15] p. Hennepin County.

The Church of the Nativity: A Short History Compiled on the Occasion of the New Church. Bloomington: The Church, 1980. 44 p. Hennepin County.

Diamond Jubilee Directory, 1896-1971. Annunciation Church, Mayhew Lake, Minnesota. N.p.: [The Church?], 1971. [40] p. German, Benton County.

Durand, Arthur H. *History of Annunciation Church of Hazelwood, Minnesota.* St. Paul: Remnant Press, [197-?]. 30 p. Rice County.

50th Jubilee, 1918-1968, Church of the Holy Family. St. Paul: The Church, 1968. [156] p. With biographical sketches. Maronite, St. Paul.

First 100 Years: St. Rose of Lima Parish, Argyle, Minnesota, 1879-1979. N.p.: Privately published, 1979. 143 p. With biographical sketches. French Canadian, Marshall County.

Gallik, George A. *Our Parish Lives: One Hundred Years, 1872-1972.* Pine City: Immaculate Conception Church, 1972. 49 p. Pine County.

Hazel, Robert. *Notre Dame de Minneapolis: The French-Canadian Catholics.* Minneapolis: Post Printing Co., 1977. 54 p.

A History of the Catholic Church in Becker, Minnesota, 1852-1952. N.p.: [The Church?, 1952]. 47 p. Sherburne County.

Immaculate Heart of Mary Church, St. Paul. *Silver Anniversary, 1949-1974.* N.p., 1974. [10] p.

Kozak, Michael J. *Ukrainians on the Minnesota Iron Range: The Story the Church Tells.* Minneapolis: Privately published, 1978. 10 p. SS. Peter and Paul's Ukrainian Catholic Church, Chisholm.

LeBlanc, Stella N. *The First Cross: Belle Prairie, Diocese of St. Cloud, Minnesota.* N.p.: Privately published, 1970. 56 p. French Canadian, Morrison County.

Sacred Heart Church [Robbinsdale]. *Commemorating the Dedication of the Sacred Heart Church Multi Purpose Building . . . June 30, 1974.* Robbinsdale: The Church, 1974. [38] p.

Sacred Heart Parish [Freeport]. *Centennial, 1881-1981: "Heritage of Faith."* Chicago, [1981?]. [134] p. Stearns County.

St. Agnes Church [St. Paul]. *50th Anniversary, One Half Century, 1887-1937, Church of St. Agnes, Saint Paul, Minnesota.* St. Paul: North Central Pub. Co., 1937. 73 p. German.

St. Ann Church: Diamond Jubilee, 1905-1980, Blackduck, Minn. Northome: The Church, 1980. [28] p. Beltrami County.

St. Anthony Parish, Lismore. *Commemorating the Golden Jubilee of St. Anthony Parish, Lismore, Minnesota, May 20, 1953.* Slayton: Murray County Herald, 1953. 68 p. Nobles County.

St. Boniface Church Centennial Committee [Cold Spring]. *Amid Hills of Granite—A Spring of Faith: A History of Saint Boniface Parish, Cold Spring, Minnesota, 1878- 1978.* Cold Spring: Record, 1978. 117 p. Stearns County.

St. Josephat's Church, Duluth. *Forty Years of Christian Service: St. Josephat's Parish, Polish National Catholic Church, Duluth, Minnesota, 1908-1948.* [Duluth?], 1948. 34 p.

St. Mary's Church, Beardsley. *Jubilee, St. Mary's Church, Beardsley, Minnesota: Seventieth Anniversary of Parish, 1884-1954, Fiftieth Anniversary of Church, 1904-1954.* N.p., 1954. 44 p. Irish, Big Stone County.

St. Stanislaus Church, Winona. *St. Stanislaus Parish, 1871-1971.* Chicago: Durand, 1971. [141] p. Polish.

St. Thomas the Apostle Parish, St. Paul. *Silver Jubilee, 1954-1979.* Chicago, 1979. [60] p.

St. Vincent de Paul Church, St. Paul. *Eightieth Anniversary Homecoming: Church of St. Vincent de Paul, St. Paul, Minnesota, September 15, 1968.* St. Paul, 1968. 56 p.

Saints Peter and Paul's Catholic Church [Duluth]. *Sts. Peter and Paul's: A Faith Community 75 Years Growing, 1901-1976. Dedication—75th Anniversary Booklet.* [Duluth], 1976. 15 p. Polish.

Schuiling, Walter J. *History of St. Philip's Parish, 1897-1975.* [Bemidji?: The Church?], 1977. 283 p. With bibliog. Bemidji.

Schumacher, Claire W. *This Is Our St. Rose Church in Proctor, Minnesota, 1898-1976: A Catholic's Viewpoint of History*. Proctor: The Church, 1976. 84 p. St. Louis County.

Scully, Leona M. *Commemorating the Golden Jubilee of Saint Columba Parish, Iona, Minnesota, June 12, 1941*. Slayton: Murray County Herald, 1941. 56 p. Murray County.

Stones and Hills—Steine und Huegel: Reflections, St. John the Baptist Parish, 1875-1975. Collegeville: The Church, 1975. 179 p. German, Stearns County.

Witte, Patricia K. *St. Marcus Parish, Clear Lake, Minnesota: Story of a Community*. [Clear Lake?]: Privately published, [1978]. 78 p. With bibliog. German, Sherburne County.

CHURCH LEADERS

Coleman, Sister Bernard and Sister Verona LaBud. *Masinaigans: The Little Book. A Biography of Monsignor Joseph F. Buh, Slovenian Missionary in America, 1864-1922*. St. Paul: North Central Pub. Co., 1972. 368 p. With bibliog. Biographical appendix lists Slovenian priests.

Hogan, Richard M. *A Minnesota Shepherd: The Most Reverend Alphonse James Schladweiler*. St. Paul: The Author, 1979. 88 p. Founding bishop of the Diocese of New Ulm.

Protestant Churches
GENERAL

Hendricks, Harry. *God at Work East of Sandstone*. N.p.: Privately published, [197-?]. 12 p. Pine County.

Pollock, John. *Billy Graham: The Authorized Biography*. New York: McGraw-Hill, 1966. President of Northwestern Schools, Minneapolis, pp. 41–46.

BAPTIST

Johnson, Dell G. "The Victory of Fundamentalism in the Minnesota Baptist Convention," in *Central Bible Quarterly*, 20:26–59 (Spring, 1977).

Minnesota Baptist Conference. *Pioneering With God's Promises: A Historical Sketch of the Minnesota Baptist Conference, 1858-1958*. St. Paul, [1958?]. 80 p.

Russell, C. Allyn. "William Bell Riley: Architect of Fundamentalism," in *MH*, 43:14–30 (Spring, 1972). Reprinted in *Foundations*, 18:26–52 (Jan.–Mar., 1975) and in C. A. Russell, *Voices of American Fundamentalism: Seven Biographical Studies*. Philadelphia: Westminster Press, 1976, pp. 79–106.

Sommerdorf, Norma. *A Church in Lowertown: The First Baptist Church of Saint Paul*. St. Paul: Mason Pub. Co., 1975. 272 p.

Swenson, Wayne. *Houston Baptist Church: The First 125 Years*. N.p.: Privately published, 1978. 36 p. Swedish, Houston County.

CONGREGATIONAL AND UNITED CHURCH OF CHRIST

First Congregational Church [Granite Falls]. *Centennial Booklet of First Congregational Church, United Church of Christ, 1872-1972*. Granite Falls, 1972. 36 p. Yellow Medicine County.

Friedens United Church of Christ [Norwood]. *100th Anniversary, Friedens United Church of Christ: "County Line Church."* Glencoe: Franklin Printing, [1980?]. 40 p. German Evangelical and Reformed, McLeod and Carver counties.

Lucas, Paul R. "The Church and the City: Congregationalism in Minneapolis, 1850–1890," in *MH*, 44:55–69 (Summer, 1974).

Peterson, Edgar A. *History of the Swedish Congregational Mission Church, North Mankato, Minn*. N.p.: Privately published, 1937. [50] p.

St. Paul's United Church of Christ, Plato, Minnesota, 1880-1980. Glencoe: The Church, [1980?]. 33 p. German Evangelical and Reformed, McLeod County.

St. Paul's United Church of Christ [St. Paul]. *The Past Is Prologue: Saint Paul's United Church of Christ, 1879-1979, Saint Paul, Minnesota*. [St. Paul?], 1979. 32 p.

South Elmdale Congregational Church, Holdingford, Minnesota, 1897-1972, 75th Anniversary. N.p.: Privately published, 1972. [12] p. Slovak, Stearns County.

LUTHERAN
General

Bergendoff, Conrad. *The Augustana Ministerium: A Study of the Careers of the 2,504 Pastors of the Augustana Evangelical Lutheran Synod/Church, 1850-1962*. Rock Island, Ill.: Augustana Historical Soc., 1980. 246 p. With bibliog.

Levang, Joseph H. *The Church of the Lutheran Brethren, 1900-1975: A Believers' Fellowship—A Lutheran Alternative*. Fergus Falls: Lutheran Brethren Pub. Co., 1980. 396 p.

German

1896-1971: Diamond Jubilee Booklet of Peace Evangelical Lutheran Church, Echo, Minnesota. N.p.: [The Church?], 1971. 43 p. Yellow Medicine County.

Evangelical Lutheran Immanuel Church, Hay Creek. *Brief History of the Ev. Luth. Immanuel's Congregation at Hay Creek, Goodhue Co., Minn.: Compiled for the Diamond Jubilee, August 27, 1933*. Lake City, 1933. [52] p.

100th Year, Trinity Lutheran Church, Janesville, Minnesota. N.p.: The Church, [1980?]. [44] p. Waseca County.

History of Trinity Evangelical Lutheran Congregation [Waconia], 1865-1940. Waconia: The Church, 1940. 29 p. Carver County.

St. John's Evangelical Lutheran Church [St. Paul]. *Our Centennial Reminiscences, 1871-1971.* Stillwater: Croixside Press, 1971. 36 p.

Trinity Lutheran Church, U.A.C. [St. Paul]. *Dedication Memorial of Trinity Lutheran Church, U.A.C.* St. Paul, 1951. 37 p.

Norwegian

Gjerde, S. S. and P. Ljostveit. *The Hauge Movement in America.* [Minneapolis]: Hauge Inner Mission Federation, 1941. Inner Mission Societies in Minn., pp. 239–279.

Kongsvinger Lutheran Church, Donnelly. *1876-1976: The First Century.* N.p., 1976. 53 p. Stevens County.

Lake Hanska Lutheran Church. *Lake Hanska Lutheran Church Centennial, 1869-1969.* N.p., 1969. 65 p. Brown County.

Norseland Lutheran Church. *100th Anniversary: Norseland Lutheran Church, St. Peter, Minnesota, 1858-1958.* N.p., 1958. 36 p. Nicollet County.

Swedish

Johnson, Emeroy. "The Archives of the Minnesota Synod of the Lutheran Church in America, of Gustavus Adolphus College, and of Minnesota College," in *Swedish Pioneer Historical Quarterly,* 29:215–217 (July, 1978).

———. *Scandian Grove: A New Look—A History of the Scandian Grove Evangelical Lutheran Church, St. Peter, Minnesota, 1858-1980.* Rev. 2nd ed. St. Peter: Church Historical Committee, 1980. 151 p. 1st ed. published 1958. Nicollet County.

Lewis, Ann. *Eternal Heritage in Christ: The Story of the First 100 Years of the Salem Lutheran Church [Dalbo] and the Surrounding Communities.* Dalbo: Church Centennial Committee, 1974. 139 p. Isanti County.

Lindquist, Ralph R. *125th Anniversary, 1854-1979: Theme, "Lead On, O King Eternal."* [St. Paul?]: First Lutheran Church, 1979. 28 p. St. Paul.

100 Years at Christ Lutheran Church, Marine on St. Croix, Minnesota. Marine on St. Croix: The Church, 1972. 34 p. Washington County.

Providence Valley Lutheran Church. *Centennial Year, 1878-1978.* Dawson, 1978. [60] p. Lac qui Parle County.

Spring Lake Evangelical Lutheran Church. *Spring Lake Lutheran, 1874-1974: 100th Anniversary.* North Branch, 1974. 152 p. Isanti County.

Other Congregations

Arlington Hills Lutheran Church [St. Paul]. *A History of Arlington Hills Lutheran Church Published on the Occasion of Its Golden Anniversary, September 30, 1959.* St. Paul, 1959. 101 p.

Carlson, Roger E. *Diamond Jubilee, St. Luke's English Lutheran Church, Goodhue, Mn., 1897-1972.* N.p.: [The Church?], 1972. [16] p.

50th Anniversary, Beautiful Savior Lutheran Church, New Hope, Minn.: History . . . 1924-1974. N.p.: [The Church?], 1974. [8] p. Finnish, Hennepin County.

Our Saviour's Lutheran Church [Canby]. *Centennial 71.* Canby, 1971. 32 p. Yellow Medicine County.

Prince of Glory Lutheran Church, Minneapolis. *50 Years Together in Ministry.* N.p., [1973]. 12 p. Slovak.

Robinson, Jean and Harry Heim. *How to Build a Church: A Somewhat Sentimentalized History of Richfield Lutheran Church During Its First Half Century, 1915-1965.* [Richfield: The Church, 1965?]. 83 p.

St. John's Centennial Committee [Elk River]. *St. John's Lutheran Church, One-Hundred Years, 1876-1976.* [Elk River, 1976]. 36 p. Sherburne County.

Urban, Thomas. *Holy Trinity Evangelical Lutheran Church, Lakefield, Jackson County, Minnesota: A Brief History Commemorating the Fiftieth Anniversary of Its Congregation, 1896-1946.* Lakefield: Standard, 1946. [23] p. Partly in Slovak.

Vandersluis, Charles, ed. *Ninety Years at St. Paul's [Icelandic Lutheran Church, Minneota].* 2 vols. Marshall: Ousman Printing, 1977–78. Lyon County.

METHODIST

Carlock, Walter. *History of Wesley United Methodist Church [Minneapolis], September 20, 1952-1977.* Minneapolis: The Church, 1977. 189 p. With biographical sketches.

Centennial Anniversary of First Methodist Church, Faribault, Minnesota, 1855-1955. N.p.: The Church, 1955. [24] p. Part of congregation was German.

Dunsworth, Richard B., ed. *A Centennial History of Hennepin Avenue United Methodist Church, 1875-1975.* [Minneapolis: The Church, 1975]. 152 p. Minneapolis.

Dyer, John L. *The Snow-Shoe Itinerant: An Autobiography.* Cincinnati: Cranston & Stowe, 1890. Richland mission, Fillmore County, and Austin circuit, pp. 69–103.

PRESBYTERIAN

Angell, Madeline and Mary C. Miller. *Joseph Woods Hancock: The Life and Times of a Minnesota Pioneer.* Minneapolis: Dillon Press, 1980. 227 p. With bibliog. Minister in Red Wing.

Bushnell, John E. *The History of Westminster Presbyterian Church of Minneapolis, Minnesota, 1907-1937.* Minneapolis: Lund Press, Inc., 1938. 169 p.

Czech Brethren Presbyterian Church, Silver Lake, Minnesota, 1876–1976. N.p.: The Church, 1976. 32 p. McLeod County.

First Presbyterian Church [Duluth]. *One Hundredth Anniversary, 1869–1969.* Duluth, 1969. 42 p.

First Presbyterian Church, Rochester. *First Presbyterian Church, Rochester, Minnesota: Centennial Celebration, 1861–1961.* Rochester, 1961. 60 p. Revision and condensation of 90th-anniversary booklet.

Kaloides, Ann G., ed. *Histories of Presbyterian Churches in the Twin Cities Area.* N.p.: Privately published, 1976. [55] p.

Kay, James. *The Way through the Wilderness: The Story of Blackduck's Presbyterians, 1900–1906.* Blackduck: American, 1976. 32 p. Beltrami County.

Morse, Stephen E. *A History of Christ United Presbyterian Church.* N.p.: [The Church?], 1978. 38 p. Marshall, Lyon County.

Oliver Presbyterian Church, Minneapolis. *Golden Jubilee, Oliver Presbyterian Church, Minneapolis, Minnesota: March 7, 1884-March 7, 1934.* N.p., 1934. [9] p.

Quist, John W. *90th Anniversary, 1888–1978, The First Presbyterian Church, Ashby, Minnesota: "People of the Covenant."* Battle Lake: Review, 1978. 40 p. Grant County.

[Thomas, William R. and others]. *Centenary History of the Jerusalem Presbyterian Church, Lake Crystal, Minnesota.* N.p.: The Church, 1958. 32 p. Welsh, Blue Earth County.

Warrendale Presbyterian Church, St. Paul. *In Commemoration of the Celebration of the Seventy-fifth Anniversary of the Founding of Warrendale Presbyterian Church, Saint Paul, Minnesota.* N.p., 1964. [14] p.

Westminster Presbyterian Church [Minneapolis]. *The History of Westminster Presbyterian Church of Minneapolis, Minnesota, and of the Celebration of Its Fiftieth Anniversary, 1857–1907.* Minneapolis: Review Pub. Co., 1907. 359 p.

Woolworth, Nancy L. *Some Historical Highlights of the Twin Cities Area Presbytery, 1829–1977.* N.p.: Presbytery of the Twin Cities Area, 1978. 14 p.

PROTESTANT EPISCOPAL

Anderson, Donald G. *A History of the Church of the Holy Communion, St. Peter, Minnesota, 1854 to 1977.* N.p.: Privately printed, 1977. 25 p. With bibliog. Nicollet County.

Christ Church, Red Wing, Minnesota, 1858–1958. N.p.: The Church, 1958. 48 p. Goodhue County.

Church of Our Saviour, Little Falls. *Silver Jubilee of the Consecration of the Church of Our Saviour, Little Falls, Minnesota.* N.p., 1935. 32 p. Morrison County.

Church of the Redeemer, Cannon Falls. *Centennial Celebration, 1857–1957.* N.p., 1957. [8] p. Goodhue County.

Clark, Lawrence S., Sr. *A Community in Christ: A Century at St. Paul's Parish [Minneapolis], 1880–1980.* Minneapolis: The Church, 1980. 61 p.

Frost, Harry J. *History of St. Matthew's Episcopal Church.* Princeton: Princeton Pub., 1979. 22 p. St. Paul.

Gethsemane Church, Minneapolis. *Parish of Gethsemane, Minneapolis, Minnesota, 1856–1906.* N.p., 1906. 50 p.

History of Calvary Episcopal Church, Rochester, Minnesota, 1860–1970. N.p.: The Church, 1970. 80 p.

Ludcke, George and Jeannette Ludcke. *A History of St. Martin's by-the-Lake Episcopal Church.* Minnetonka Beach: The Church, 1978. 92 p. Hennepin County.

Reed, Robert R. *A Centennial Memorial Album, 1856–1956.* Winona: St. Paul's Episcopal Church, 1956. 79 p.

Sheppard, Edward L. *The Second Fifty Years: The Diocese of Minnesota and the Diocese of Duluth from 1907 to 1957.* Minneapolis: Diocese of Minn., 1972. 114 p. With bibliog.

OTHER PROTESTANT CHURCHES

Brookdale Covenant Church. *Seventy-Five Years Serving Christ in the Camden and Brooklyn Center Area, 1899–1974.* Minneapolis: The Church, 1974. 47 p. Hennepin County.

Evangelical Church, Minnesota Conference. *75th Anniversary Advance, Minnesota Conference, Evangelical Church, 1942–1943.* [St. Paul?], 1942. [24] p.

First Covenant Church, Minneapolis. *Forward in Faith: Centennial '74.* N.p., 1974. [72] p. Swedish.

Greenleafton Reformed Church [Preston]. *One Hundredth Anniversary: Greenleafton Reformed Church, Preston, Minnesota, 1867–1967.* N.p.: Privately published, 1967. 28 p. Dutch, Fillmore County.

Jones, Edith H. *History of Minneapolis Friends Meeting, 1863–1963.* N.p.: Privately published, [196–?]. 7 p.

Otto, Elinor S. *The Story of Unity Church, 1872–1972.* St. Paul: The Church, 1972. 130 p. With bibliog. Unitarian, St. Paul.

Sandvik, Marie and Doris Nye. *To the Slums with Love: 30 Years Bringing God's Love to the Inner City.* Minneapolis: Marie Sandvik Center, [1971?]. 78 p. Formerly Minneapolis Revival Mission.

[Schrader, Lydia C.]. "Our Church in St. Paul," in *The Messenger* (Kitchener, Ont.), vol. 197, no. 13, pp. 19, 21 (Jan., 1977). Swedenborgian.

Thorwall, LaReau. *. . . And Light New Fires: The Story of Axel Johnson Thorwall, an Immigrant Blacksmith who Exchanged His Forge for a Frock*

Coat. Minneapolis: Free Church Publications, 1969. 186 p. Evangelical Free Church of America.

Trapp, D. C. *The History of the Evangelical Church in Minneapolis.* N.p.: Privately published, 1935. 6 p.

Weeldreyer, M. *Fiftieth Anniversary of the Bethany Reformed Church, Clara City, Minnesota.* Clara City: Herald, 1939. 34 p. East Frisian, Chippewa County.

THE ARTS
General

Koplos, Janet, ed. *Crafts in Minnesota.* Minneapolis: School of Journalism and Mass Communication, Univ. of Minn., 1976. 48 p.

Lofgren, John Z. *The American Swedish Institute: Collections and Swan J. Turnblad Mansion.* Minneapolis: The Institute, 1979. 48 p.

Rahm, Virginia L. "Human Hair Ornaments," in *MH*, 44:70–74 (Summer, 1974).

Schwarz, Ann. *Rochester Art Center: Growth and Development.* Rochester: The Center, [1979]. 11 p.

Sherman, John K. *Art and Culture in Minneapolis.* Minneapolis: Chamber of Commerce, [1964?]. [48] p.

Westbrook, Nicholas and Carolyn Gilman. "Minnesota Patchwork," in *MH*, 46:237–245 (Summer, 1979). Quilt exhibit.

White, John F. "The University of Minnesota Gallery and the New Deal: A Lesson in Creative Partnership," in Midwest Museums Conference, *Quarterly,* vol. 40, nos. 1, 2, pp. 13–19 (Winter/Spring, 1980).

Architecture
GENERAL

Brooks, H. Allen. *The Prairie School: Frank Lloyd Wright and His Midwest Contemporaries.* Univ. of Toronto Press, 1972. Purcell, Feick and Elmslie, pp. 201–227.

Cowles, Linn Ann and Peter Johnson. *The Work of Purcell and Elmslie in Saint Paul and Minneapolis, Minnesota.* Hopkins: Greenwich Design, 1978. [32] p., map. Mostly Minneapolis.

Doumato, Lamia. *Cass Gilbert, 1859–1934.* (Architecture Series: Bibliography.) Monticello, Ill.: Vance Bibliographies, 1980. 10 p.

Ellerbe, Thomas F. *The Ellerbe Tradition: Seventy Years of Architecture & Engineering.* Ed. by Bonnie Richter. Minneapolis: Ellerbe, Inc., 1980. 144 p.

Gebhard, David and Tom Martinson. *A Guide to the Architecture of Minnesota.* Minneapolis: Univ. of Minn. Press, 1977. 469 p. With bibliog. and illustrations.

Gimmestad, Dennis A. and James K. Nestingen. *Five Redwood County Towns: An Architectural Survey of Lucan, Milroy, Sanborn, Wabasso, Walnut Grove.* Lucan: Rural Cities Administration, 1977. 133 p. With bibliog.

Larson, Philip. *World Architecture in Minnesota: A Generation of Historical Revival, 1890–1930. An Exhibition Organized by Minnesota Landmarks.* St. Paul: Minnesota Landmarks, 1979. 43 p.

Lathrop, Alan K. "Emmanuel L. Masqueray, 1861–1917," in *MH*, 47:43–56 (Summer, 1980).

Michels, Eileen M. *An Architectural View: 1883–1974. The Minneapolis Society of Fine Arts.* Minneapolis: The Society, 1974. [52] p.

———. *Edwin Hugh Lundie, F.A.I.A. (1886–1972): A Comprehensive Exhibition of Architectural Drawings, Renderings and Photographs.* St. Paul: Minnesota Museum of Art, 1972. [24] p.

———. *A Landmark Reclaimed: The Federal Building, 1902; The Old Federal Courts Building, 1965; The Landmark Center, 1972, of St. Paul.* St. Paul: Minnesota Landmarks, 1977. 111 p.

Minnesota Historical Society and Minnesota State Planning Agency. *Historic Preservation for Minnesota Communities.* St. Paul, 1980. 64 p. With bibliog.

Northwest Architectural Archives. *Purcell and Elmslie, Architects: Chicago, Philadelphia, Minneapolis.* Minneapolis, 1976. [8] p. Exhibition pamphlet.

Ramsey, Ronald L., ed. *Fargo-Moorhead: A Guide to Historic Architecture.* [Fargo]: Plains Architectural Heritage Foundation, 1975. Moorhead and Kragnes, pp. 57–75, 82, 83.

Saint Anthony Falls Rediscovered. Minneapolis: Riverfront Development Coordination Board, 1980. 129 p. Photographs and panorama map.

St. Paul Planning Dept. *Saint Paul Architecture.* St. Paul, 1975. 60 p. With bibliog.

Scott, James A. *Duluth's Legacy.* Vol. 1. *Architecture.* Duluth: Dept. of Research & Planning, 1974. 165 p.

Skrief, Charles W. "The Summit Avenue Case," in *MH*, 46:75–77 (Summer, 1978).

Tselos, Dimitris. "The Enigma of Buffington's Skyscraper," in *Art Bulletin*, 26:3–12 (Mar., 1944).

Warn, Robert R. "Bennett & Sullivan, Client & Creator," in *Prairie School Review*, 10:1–3, 5–15 (3rd quarter, 1973); "Louis H. Sullivan, '. . . An Air of Finality'," 10:1–3, 5–19, 27 (4th quarter, 1973). With bibliog. 1st part of this 2-part article is an elaboration of "Two House Projects for the Carl K. Bennett Family [of Owatonna] by Louis Sullivan and Purcell & Elmslie," in *Northwest Architect*, 36:64–72 (Mar.–Apr., 1972).

Western Architect. *The Work of Purcell and Elmslie, Architects; with a New Introd. by David Gebhard . . . includes All of the Text and Plates Originally Contained in the Pages of the January 1913, January 1915 and July 1915 Issues of The Western Architect.*

Park Forest, Ill.: Prairie School Press, 1965. 96 p. Reprinted in H. Allen Brooks, ed. *Prairie School Architecture: Studies from 'The Western Architect.'* Univ. of Toronto Press, 1975, pp. 46–129.

RELIGIOUS

Amussen, Diane, ed. *The House of Hope Presbyterian Church.* St. Paul: The Church, 1976. 63 p.

Lavine, Marcia and Thomas Williams. *Saint John's Furniture, 1874–1974.* Collegeville: St. John's Abbey, 1974. 19 p. Exhibition catalog.

DOMESTIC

Karni, Michael and Robert Levin. "Northwoods Vernacular Architecture: Finnish Log Building in Minnesota," in *Northwest Architecture,* 36:92–99 (May-June, 1972).

Kaups, Matti. "A Finnish *Riihi* in Minnesota," in *Minn. Academy of Science, Journal,* 38:66–71 (1972). With bibliog. Barn construction near Eveleth, St. Louis County.

——. "A Finnish Savusauna in Minnesota," in *MH,* 45:11–20 (Spring, 1976). In Kalevala Township, Carlton County.

Peterson, Fred W. *Western Minnesota Architecture, 1870–1900.* Morris: Univ. of Minn., n.d. [27] p. With bibliog.

Literature
GENERAL

Ervin, Jean, ed. *The Minnesota Experience: An Anthology.* Minneapolis: Adams Press, 1979. Introd., pp. 9–29, and bibliog., pp. 451–455. Fiction set in Minn.

Lång, Helmer. "Moberg, the Emigrant Saga and Reality," in *Swedish Pioneer Historical Quarterly,* 23:3–24 (Jan., 1972).

McKnight, Roger. *Moberg's Emigrant Novels and the Journals of Andrew Peterson: A Study of Influences and Parallels.* New York: Arno Press, 1979. 235 p.

Norelius, Theodore A. "Memories of Vilhelm Moberg at Chisago Lakes," in *Swedish Pioneer Historical Quarterly,* 30:53–59 (Jan., 1979).

MINNESOTA AUTHORS

Anderson, Chester G., ed. *Growing Up in Minnesota: Ten Writers Remember Their Childhoods.* Minneapolis: Univ. of Minn. Press, 1976. 250 p. The authors are Meridel Le Sueur, Harrison E. Salisbury, Gerald Vizenor, Keith Gunderson, Shirley Schoonover, Toyse Kyle, Robert Bly, Edna and Howard Hong, and Mary Hong Loe.

Becker, Muriel R. *Clifford D. Simak: A Primary and Secondary Bibliography.* Boston: G. K. Hall and Co., 1980. 149 p. Editor and columnist for *Minneapolis Tribune* and *Star* and author of science fiction.

Bruccoli, Matthew J. *F. Scott Fitzgerald: A Descriptive Bibliography.* (Pittsburgh Series in Bibliography.) Univ. of Pittsburgh Press, 1972. 369 p.

——. *Some Sort of Epic Grandeur: The Life of F. Scott Fitzgerald.* New York: Harcourt Brace Jovanovich, 1981. 624 p. With bibliog. of Fitzgerald's writings.

——. *Supplement to F. Scott Fitzgerald: A Descriptive Bibliography.* Univ. of Pittsburgh Press, 1980. 219 p.

—— and Margaret M. Duggan, eds. *Correspondence of F. Scott Fitzgerald.* New York: Random House, 1980. 640 p.

Buckley, Joan N. "Martha Ostenso: A Norwegian–American Immigrant Novelist," in Norwegian–Am. Historical Assn., *Studies,* 28:69–81 (1979). Ostenso's use of Norwegian themes.

Dorfman, Joseph. *Thorstein Veblen and His America.* New York: Viking Press, 1934. 556 p. With bibliog. of Veblen's works.

Flora, Joseph M. *Frederick Manfred.* Boise: Boise State Univ., 1974. 52 p. Literary criticism.

Galbraith, John K. "A New Theory of Thorstein Veblen," in *American Heritage,* 24:32–40 (Apr., 1973).

Huseboe, Arthur R. and William Geyer, eds. *Where the West Begins: Essays on Middle Border and Siouxland Writing in Honor of Herbert Krause.* Sioux Falls, S.D.: Center for Western Studies Press, Augustana College, 1978. 160 p. Essays on Frederick Manfred, Ole Rølvaag, Robert Bly, Laura Ingalls Wilder, and Scandinavian immigrant fiction.

Kane, Patricia. "F. Scott Fitzgerald's St. Paul: A Writer's Use of Material," in *MH,* 45:141–148 (Winter, 1976).

Koblas, John J. *F. Scott Fitzgerald in Minnesota: His Homes and Haunts.* (Minn. Historic Sites Pamphlet 18.) St. Paul: MHS, 1978. 41 p.

Love, Glen A. "New Pioneering on the Prairies: Nature, Progress and the Individual in the Novels of Sinclair Lewis," in *American Quarterly,* 25:558–577 (Dec., 1973).

Manfred, Frederick F. *Conversations with Frederick Manfred.* Moderated by John R. Milton. Salt Lake City: Univ. of Utah Press, 1974. 169 p.

Neidle, Cecyle S. *Great Immigrants.* New York: Twayne, 1973. Ole E. Rølvaag, pp. 181–202.

Patterson, John. "From Yeoman to Beast: Images of Blackness in [Ignatius Donnelly's] *Caesar's Column,*" in *American Studies,* 12:21–31 (Fall, 1971).

Qualey, Carlton C., ed. *Thorstein Veblen: The Carleton College Veblen Seminar Essays.* New York: Columbia Univ. Press, 1968. 170 p. With bibliog. of Veblen's works.

Ray, Jo Anne. "Maud Hart Lovelace and Mankato," in Barbara Stuhler and Gretchen Kreuter, eds., *Women* of *Minnesota: Selected Biographical Essays.* St. Paul: MHS, 1977, pp. 155–172.

Rippley, La Vern J. "Alexander Berghold, Pioneer Priest and Prairie Poet," in *Currents,* vol. 2, no. 2, pp. 16–31 (Fall, 1979).

Ruud, Curtis D. "Beret and the Prairie in *Giants in the Earth,*" in Norwegian–Am. Historical Assn., *Studies,* 28:217–244 (1979). Ole E. Rølvaag's analysis of the immigrant experience on the prairies.

Stefanik, Ernest C., Jr. *John Berryman: A Descriptive Bibliography.* (Pittsburgh Series in Bibliography.) Univ. of Pittsburgh Press, 1974. 316 p.

Thorson, Gerald. "Tinsel and Dust: Disenchantment in Two Minneapolis Novels from the 1880s," in *MH,* 45:210–222 (Summer, 1977). The subjects are *En Saloonkeepers datter,* by Drude K. Janson, and *Bag Gardinet* (Behind the Curtain), by Kristofer Janson (both in Norwegian).

———, ed. *Ole Rølvaag: Artist and Cultural Leader: Papers Presented at the Rølvaag Symposium held at St. Olaf College, October 28–29, 1974.* Northfield: St. Olaf College Press, 1975. 74 p. With bibliog.

Zochert, Donald. *Laura: The Life of Laura Ingalls Wilder.* Chicago: Contemporary Books, 1976. Walnut Grove, pp. 127–146.

Music

Carlson, Bruce. "Schubert Club History Reflects Romance of Music in St. Paul," in *Ramsey County History,* vol. 10, no. 2, pp. 3–12 (Fall, 1973). Background and origins of the club.

Dunn, James T. "A Century of Song: Popular Music in Minnesota," in *MH,* 44:122–141 (Winter, 1974).

Flanagan, Barbara. *Ovation: A Partnership between a Great Orchestra and a Great Audience.* Minneapolis: The Minn. Orchestra, 1977. 132 p.

Johnston, Patricia C. "Making Music," in *Roots,* vol. 9, no. 1 (Fall, 1980). 31 p.

Thompson, Toby. *Positively Main Street: An Unorthodox View of Bob Dylan.* New York: Coward–McCann, 1971. 187 p. His Minn. background.

Painting, Drawing, and Sculpture

GENERAL

Coen, Rena N. *Painting and Sculpture in Minnesota, 1820–1914.* Minneapolis: Univ. of Minn. Press, 1976. 146 p. With bibliog. Includes Ellen W. Bauer, "Appendix: Painters and Sculptors Associated with Minnesota, 1820–1914," pp. 132–137.

Highwater, Jamake. *The Sweet Grass Lives On: Fifty Contemporary North American Indian Artists.* New York: Lippincott and Crowell, 1980. 192 p. With bibliog. Includes Carl Gawboy and George Morrison.

Johnson, Nancy A. *Accomplishments: Minnesota Art Projects in the Depression Years.* Duluth: Tweed Museum of Art, Univ. of Minn., 1976. 39 p. With bibliog. Exhibition catalog.

Keim, Rebecca L. *Three Women Artists: [Wanda] Gag, [Frances] Greenman, and [Clara] Mairs.* Minneapolis: Univ. Gallery, Univ. of Minn., 1980. 34 p. Exhibition catalog with biographical sketches.

Nord, Mary Ann. "Artists At Work," in *Roots,* vol. 8, no. 2 (Winter, 1980). 31 p.

INDIVIDUAL ARTISTS
(Arranged alphabetically by artist)

Anderson, Marilyn B. "Carl L. Boeckmann: Norwegian Artist in the New World," in Norwegian–Am. Historical Assn., *Studies,* 28:309–323 (1979). Manager of T. B. Walker's art gallery in Minneapolis, 1908–23.

Archabal, Nina M. "In Memoriam, Cameron Booth, 1892–1980: A Chronicle from His Scrapbooks," in *MH,* 47:100–110 (Fall, 1980). Illustrations from MHS Collections.

Johnston, Patricia C. "Edward Brewer: Illustrator and Portrait Painter," in *MH,* 47:3–15 (Spring, 1980).

Coen, Rena N. "Alfred Thompson Bricher's Early Minnesota Scenes," in *MH,* 46:233–236 (Summer, 1979).

Cox, Richard [W.]. "Adolph Dehn: Satirist of the Jazz Age," in Archives of Am. Art, *Journal,* vol. 18, no. 2, pp. 11–18 (1978).

———. "Adolf Dehn: The Minnesota Connection," in *MH,* 45:166–186 (Spring, 1977).

Eastman, Seth. *Seth Eastman's Mississippi: A Lost Portfolio Recovered.* [Ed. by] John F. McDermott. Urbana: Univ. of Illinois Press, 1973. 149 p. With bibliog.

Lindemann, Edna M., ed. *Alexis Jean Fournier: A Barbizon in East Aurora.* Buffalo: State Univ. College, 1979. 11 p. Exhibition catalog.

Klammer, Paul W. *Wanda Gag, an Artist of Distinct Individuality.* New Ulm: Brown County Historical Soc., 1979. 18 p.

Cox, Richard W. "Wanda Gág: The Bite of the Picture Book," in *MH,* 44:238–254 (Fall, 1975).

Hancock, Jane. *Clement Haupers: Six Decades of Art in Minnesota.* St. Paul: MHS, 1979. 32 p. Exhibition catalog.

Westbrook, Nicholas, ed. "Clement Haupers: Conversations on Six Decades of Painting in Minnesota," in *MH,* 46:296–299 (Fall, 1979). Reminiscences of his work with WPA art project.

Meister, Mark. "The Man Who Painted the Lake Gervais Tornado," in *MH,* 45:329–332 (Winter, 1977). Julius O. Holm.

Jaques, Florence P. *Francis Lee Jaques: Artist of the Wilderness World.* Garden City, N.Y.: Doubleday, 1973. 370 p.

Larson, Robert G. "Francis Lee Jaques—Interpreter of Nature's Realm," in Midwest Museums Conference, *Quarterly*, vol. 34, no. 2, pp. 14–20 (Spring, 1974).

Hills, Patricia. *Eastman Johnson*. New York: Clarkson N. Potter, Inc., 1972. With bibliog. Minn., pp. 21–29.

Gunderson, Harvey L. "Leslie C. Kouba—The Man," in *Naturalist*, vol. 31, no. 3, pp. 6–10 (Autumn, 1980).

Rudd, Clayton G. "The Artistry of Leslie C. Kouba," in *Naturalist*, vol. 31, no. 3, p. 2 (Autumn, 1980).

Page, Jean J. "Frank Blackwell Mayer: Painter of the Minnesota Indian," in *MH*, 46:66–74 (Summer, 1978).

Buck, Anita, ed. *Jo: Stillwater Bicentennial Art Project*. Stillwater: Croixside Press, 1976. [103] p. Exhibition catalog. Jo Lutz Rollins' water colors of Stillwater houses.

Schulz, Charles M. *Peanuts Jubilee: My Life and Art with Charlie Brown and Others*. New York: Holt, Rinehart and Winston, 1975. Minn. beginnings, pp. 11–36.

Montgomery, Feodora L. *My Father, Feodor Von Luerzer*. N.p.: The Author, [1973?]. 31 p.

Norton, Bettina A. *Edwin Whitefield: Nineteenth-Century North American Scenery*. Barre, Mass.: Barre Pub., 1977. 158 p. With bibliog. Illustrations.

Photography

Johnston, Patricia C. "Truman Ingersoll: St. Paul Photographer Pictured the World," in *MH*, 47:123–132 (Winter, 1980).

Martin, Virginia L. "The Eye of Brechet," in *MH*, 45: 241–244 (Summer, 1977). Mostly turn of the century photographs by Joseph J. Brechet, Glencoe.

Press Photography: Minnesota since 1930. An Exhibition organized by Walker Art Center 11 December 1977—22 January 1978. Minneapolis: The Center, 1977. 68 p. With bibliog.

St. Clair, Carol. "Flaten/Wange: Photographers," in *Red River Valley Historian*, Winter, 1978–79, pp. 23–37. Mainly photographs by O. E. Flaten of Moorhead and S. P. Wange of Hawley.

Theater

Forsyth, James. *Tyrone Guthrie: A Biography*. London: Hamish Hamilton, 1976. 372 p.

Leavitt, Dinah L. *Feminist Theatre Groups*. Jefferson, N.C.: McFarland & Co., 1980. 153 p. With bibliog. Four Minneapolis companies.

Leipold, L. Edmond. *Eddie Shipstad, Ice Follies Star*. (Men of Achievement Series.) Minneapolis: T. S. Denison, 1971. 162 p.

Mississippi Melodie: Showboat's First Twenty-Five Years at Grand Rapids, Minnesota. Grand Rapids: Northprint Co., 1980. [23] p. Illustrated.

Rossi, Alfred. *Astonish Us in the Morning: Tyrone Guthrie Remembered*. Detroit: Wayne State Univ. Press, 1980. 310 p.

Rothfuss, Herman E. "Criticism of the German–American Theater in Minnesota," in *Germanic Review*, 27: 124–130 (Apr., 1952). Reprinted, Don H. Tolzmann, ed., *German–American Literature*. Metuchen, N.J.: Scarecrow Press, 1977, pp. 98–105.

"When Stars 'Fell' on Minnesota," in *MH*, 44:108–112 (Fall, 1974). Mostly photographs of movie stars' visit to the Twin Cities, 1942.

Whiting, Frank M. *One of Us Amateurs*. Provo, Utah: Stevenson's Genealogical Center, 1980. 115 p. Autobiography; theater in the Twin Cities.

Zeigler, Joseph W. *Regional Theatre: The Revolutionary Stage*. Minneapolis: Univ. of Minn. Press, 1973. Guthrie Theater, Minneapolis, pp. 62–76 and *passim*.

CLUBS AND ORGANIZATIONS

Edgar, William C. and Loring M. Staples. *The Minneapolis Club: A Review of Its History: 1883 to 1920, by William C. Edgar, 1920 to 1974, by Loring M. Staples*. Minneapolis: The Club, 1974. 161 p. Edgar's section first published in Minneapolis Club, [*Year Book, 1920*], pp. 53–109 (1920).

Freemasons, Carnelian Lodge No. 40, Lake City. *Centennial, 1863–1963, Carnelian Lodge, No. 40, Ancient Free and Accepted Masons, Lake City, Minnesota*. Lake City: Graphic, 1963. [16] p.

Freemasons, Wayzata Lodge No. 205, Wayzata. *Souvenir Booklet, Seventy-fifth Anniversary, Wayzata Lodge No. 205. A.F. & A.M., Wayzata, Minnesota, 1893–1968*. N.p., 1968. [16] p.

Miler, Michael F. "Boy Scouts in Hennepin County," in *Hennepin County History*, vol. 36, no. 4, pp. 3–12 (Winter, 1976–77).

Minikahda Club, Minneapolis. *Minikahda Club, 75th Anniversary, 1898–1973*. N.p., 1973. 64 p.

Rahm, Virginia L. "The Nushka Club," in *MH*, 43:303–307 (Winter, 1973).

Sutherland, Katherine S. " 'Something for the Girls' of Hennepin County: The Greater Minneapolis Girl Scout Council, 1915–," in *Hennepin County History*, vol. 35, no. 1, pp. 3–13 (Winter, 1975–76).

HOLIDAYS AND SPORTS
Holidays

Muellerleile, Alfred G. *Alfred's Christmas: Reminiscences of a Childhood Christmas*. St. Paul: North Central Pub. Co., 1975. 52 p.

Qualey, Carlton C. "Independence Centennial, 1876," in *MH*, 44:223 (Summer, 1975).

Sports
GENERAL

Hess, Jeffrey A. "Sports in Minnesota," in *Roots*, vol. 8, no. 3 (Spring, 1980). 31 p.

Johnson, Charles. *History of the Metropolitan Stadium and Sports Center*. Minneapolis: Midwest Federal, [1970]. 32 p. Bloomington.

Tucker, Dunstan and Martin Schirber. *Scoreboard: A History of Athletics at St. John's University, Collegeville, Minnesota*. Collegeville: St. John's Univ. Press, 1979. 444 p.

BASEBALL AND FOOTBALL

Akers, Tom and Sam Akers. *The Game Breaker: The Story of Bruce Smith, Minnesota's Only Heisman Award Winner*. Wayzata: Ralph Turtinen Pub. Co., 1977. 176 p.

Carew, Rod and Ira Berkow. *Carew*. New York: Simon and Schuster, 1979. 251 p. Minnesota Twins.

Finch, Robert L. and others, eds. *The Story of Minor League Baseball*. Columbus, Ohio: National Assn. of Professional Baseball Leagues, 1952. 744 p. Minneapolis and St. Paul, *passim*.

McCallum, John D. *Big Ten Football Since 1895*. Radnor, Pa.: Chilton Book Co., 1976. 318 p. Univ. of Minn., *passim*.

Morlock, Bill and Rick Little. *Split Doubleheader: An Unauthorized History of the Minnesota Twins*. N.p.: Morick, 1979. 117 p.

Rainbolt, Richard. *Gold Glory . . . the Remarkable Men Who Lifted [University of] Minnesota Football into its Golden Eras*. Wayzata: Ralph Turtinen Pub. Co., 1972. 199 p.

———. *The Minnesota Vikings: A Pictorial Drama*. Minneapolis: Nodin Press, 1973. 151 p.

Swanson, Wally. *20 Years on the St. Paul Sandlots: A Story of Sports and Life in the 20's and 30's*. N.p.: Privately published, [1970?]. 112 p. Amateur football and baseball.

OTHER SPORTS

Buckanaga, Charles V. *The American Indian Boxers of Minnesota—Migodeinniwug*. Ponsford: Pine Point Pub., 1979. 192 p. Golden Gloves competition, 1919–79.

Fischler, Stan. *The Blazing North Stars*. Englewood Cliffs, N.J.: Prentice–Hall, 1972. 144 p. Hockey.

Frost, Gale C. *Thunder in the North, 1980 Edition: A Scrapbook of Speed*. St. Paul: Branston House, Inc., 1980. 105 p. Racing cars and airplanes and the people who raced them.

Jacobs, Linda. *Cindy Nelson, North Country Skier*. St. Paul: EMC Corp., 1976. 40 p. Winner of the 1974 World Cup competition.

Kelley, James E. *Minnesota Golf: 75 Years of Tournament History*. Minneapolis: O. H. Dahlen Co., 1976. 288 p.

Kerr, John. *Curling in Canada and the United States: A Record of the Tour of the Scottish Team, 1902–3, and of the Game in the Dominion and the Republic*. Edinburgh, Scot.: Geo. A. Morton, 1904. 790 p. An account of the team's visit to St. Paul and Minneapolis, pp. 633–647.

Lager, Harold E. "Skiing: 'From Necessity to Pleasure',", in *Range History*, vol. 4, no. 1, pp. 1–5 (Mar., 1979). Further notes on skiing, pp. 5, 6.

Roney, Betty. *Stillwater Country Club, 1924–1974*. N.p.: Privately published, 1974. 28 p. Golf.

Solz, Art, Jr. *Minnesota State High School Hockey Tournament History: Complete Records, Statistics, Summaries, 1945 to 1968*. Minneapolis: Privately published, [1968]. 92 p.

"Tough Times—The Sometime Fortunes of Boxing in Early Minnesota," in *Ramsey County History*, vol. 13, no. 2, pp. 13–18 (Spring/Summer, 1977). Mainly St. Paul.

See also Natural History and Conservation—Flora and Fauna (for Fishing and Hunting)

HEALTH AND MEDICINE
General

Courage Center, Golden Valley. *The Challenge of Change: Courage Center's Fifty Years*. N.p., [1979?]. 16 p.

Drought, Warren W. *Medical History: Otter Tail County, Minnesota, 1870–1940*. N.p.: Privately published, [1940?]. [16] p.

Gaarder, Pat and Tracey Baker. *From Stripes to Whites: A History of the Swedish Hospital School of Nursing, 1899–1973*. Minneapolis: Swedish Hospital Alumnae Assn., 1980. 106 p.

Green, Ellen B. "Minnesota Medicine Bag," in *Roots*, vol. 8, no. 1 (Fall, 1979). 31 p.

Macrae, Jean M. *New Hope, New Life, New Joy: The Story of the Nat G. Polinsky Memorial Rehabilitation Center, Inc. . . . Duluth . . . 1950–1975*. N.p.: Privately published, 1975. 18 p. Occupational therapy.

North-West Dentistry, vol. 37, no. 2 (March, 1958). 75th–anniversary issue.

Uphoff, Mary Jo and Walter Uphoff. *Group Health: An American Success Story in Prepaid Health Care*. Minneapolis: Dillon Press, 1980. 173 p. Legal questions involved in co-operative health care.

Medical Practice

Adair, Fred L. *The Country Doctor and the Specialist*. Maitland, Fla.: Adair Award Fund, 1968. Education and practice in Minneapolis, pp. 52–57, 65–84.

Albertson, Don L. "Sister [Elizabeth] Kenny's Legacy," in *Hennepin County History*, vol. 37, no. 1, pp. 3–14 (Spring, 1978).

Cohn, Victor. *Sister Kenny: The Woman Who Challenged the Doctors*. Minneapolis: Univ. of Minn. Press, 1975. Minn., *passim*.

Lowe, Thomas A. *Image of a Doctor*. Minneapolis: T. S. Denison, 1974. 63 p. Reminiscences.

Sanford, James A. *A General Practitioner Speaks*. N.p.: Privately published, 1954. 84 p. Reminiscences.

Thomson, Mildred. *Dr. Arthur C. Rogers: Pioneer Leader in Minnesota's Program for the Mentally Retarded*. [Minneapolis]: Minn. Assn. for Retarded Children, [196–?]. 36 p.

Hospitals and Clinics
MAYO CLINIC

Alvarez, Walter C. *Alvarez on Alvarez*. San Francisco: Strawberry Hill Press, 1977. 152 p. Reminiscences.

Guthrie, Charles M. "The Road Agent and the Doctor," in *Montana: The Magazine of Western History*, 23: 42–47 (Jan., 1973). Henry S. Plummer.

Mayo, Charles W. *Mayo: The Story of My Family and My Career*. Garden City, N.Y.: Doubleday, 1968. 351 p.

Nourse, Alan E. *Inside the Mayo Clinic*. New York: McGraw–Hill, 1979. 262 p. Every other chapter relates aspects of the clinic's history.

OTHER HOSPITALS

[Buck, Anita]. *Lakeview Memorial Hospital, Stillwater, Minnesota: Centennial of Care, 1880–1980*. Stillwater: [The Hospital?], 1980. [7] p.

Minneapolis Maternity Hospital. *Maternity Hospital, 1887–1937*. Minneapolis, 1938. 24 p.

Rønning, N[ils] N. and W. H. Lien. *The Lutheran Deaconess Home and Hospital: Fiftieth Anniversary, 1889–1939*. Minneapolis: The Home, 1939. 94 p.

St. Joseph's Hospital, St. Paul. *History of St. Joseph's Hospital, 1853–1978*. St. Paul, 1979. 63 p.

Stanchfield, Margaret A. *A History of the Variety Club Heart Hospital of the University of Minnesota Hospitals*. [Minneapolis?: The Hospital?, 1976?]. 72 p.

Veterans Administration Hospital, St. Cloud. *Fifty Years of Service to Those Who Served, 1924–1974: History of the Veterans Administration Hospital, St. Cloud, Mn*. St. Cloud, 1974. [42] p.

SOCIAL QUESTIONS
Social Welfare

Garvey, Timothy J. "The Duluth Homesteads: A Successful Experiment in Community Housing," in *MH*, 46:2–16 (Spring, 1978).

Gilman, Elizabeth. "Catheryne Cooke Gilman: Social Worker," in Barbara Stuhler and Gretchen Kreuter, eds., *Women of Minnesota: Selected Biographical Essays*. St. Paul: MHS, 1977, pp. 190–207.

Hoffman, William. *Neighborhood House, 1897–1972: A Brief History of the First 75 Years*. [St. Paul: The House?], 1972. [21] p.

Michels, Eileen M. "Alice O'Brien: Volunteer and Philanthropist," in Barbara Stuhler and Gretchen Kreuter, eds., *Women of Minnesota: Selected Biographical Essays*. St. Paul: MHS, 1977, pp. 136–154.

Pfleger, Helen W. "Volstead and Prohibition: A Roaring '20's Memoir," in *Ramsey County History*, vol. 12, no. 1, pp. 19–22 (Spring/Summer, 1975). Prohibition office in St. Paul.

St. Paul Foundation. *A History of the Saint Paul Foundation, 1940–1980*. St. Paul, 1980. [16] p.

Weiner, Lynn. " 'Our Sister's Keepers': The Minneapolis Woman's Christian Association and Housing for Working Women," in *MH*, 46:189–200 (Spring, 1979).

Wellstone, Paul D. *How the Rural Poor Got Power: Narrative of a Grass–Roots Organizer*. Amherst: Univ. of Massachusetts Press, 1978. 227 p. In Rice County.

Women and the Aged

Barsness, Diana. "Anna Ramsey: 'Shining Exemplar' of the True Woman," in *MH*, 45:258–272 (Fall, 1977).

Beito, Gretchen. *Women of Thief River Falls at the Turn of the Century: A Study of Life in a Boom Town, 1895–1905*. Thief River Falls: Pennington County Historical Soc., 1977. 40 p.

Buswell, Beulah. *Watkins United Methodist Home, Winona, Minnesota*. [Winona?]: The Home, [1979?]. 16 p.

Kreuter, Gretchen. "Kate Donnelly versus the Cult of True Womanhood," in Barbara Stuhler and Gretchen Kreuter, eds., *Women of Minnesota: Selected Biographical Essays*. St. Paul: MHS, 1977, pp. 20–33. A shorter version, "Kate Donnelly and the 'Cult of True Womanhood'," appeared in *Ramsey County History*, vol. 13, no. 2, pp. 14–18 (Fall/Winter, 1976).

Rikkinen, Kalevi and Arnold Alanen. "Migration Trends of Older Aged Persons in Minnesota," in *Acta Geographica* (Helsinki, Fin.), 21:1–17 (1970).

Thygeson, Sylvie. "In the Parlor," in Sherna Gluck, ed., *From Parlor to Prison: Five American Suffragists Talk about Their Lives*. New York: Vintage Books, 1976. Birth control movement in St. Paul, pp. 30–58.

Whiting, Eleanor. *A Biographical Sketch of Anna Jenks Ramsey: Wife of Minnesota's First Territorial Governor*. N.p.: National Soc. of the Colonial Dames of Am. in the State of Minn., n.d. 14 p.

Labor Legislation and the Labor Movement

Asher, Robert. "The Origins of Workmen's Compensation in Minnesota," in *MH*, 44:142–153 (Winter, 1974).

Dobbs, Farrell. *Teamster Bureaucracy*. New York: Monad Press, 1977. 304 p.

———. *Teamster Politics*. New York: Monad Press, 1975. 256 p.

———. *Teamster Power*. New York: Monad Press, 1973. 255 p.

———. *Teamster Rebellion*. New York: Monad Press, 1972. 190 p. Dobbs's books deal with the Trotskyist-led teamsters' union movement in the 1930s mostly in Minneapolis.

Englemann, Larry D. " 'We Were the Poor People'—The Hormel Strike of 1933," in *Labor History*, 15:483–510 (Fall, 1974).

"Joining Together: Labor Organization in Minnesota," in *Roots*, vol. 3, no. 3 (Spring, 1975). 39 p.

Minneapolis Typographical Union No. 42. *A Century of Service: Minneapolis Typographical Union No. 42, 1873–1973*. [Minneapolis?], 1973. 57 p.

Trimble, Steve. *Education & Democracy: A History of the Minneapolis Federation of Teachers*. Minneapolis: The Federation, 1979. 72 p.

Tselos, George. "Self–Help and Sauerkraut: The Organized Unemployed, Inc., of Minneapolis," in *MH*, 45:306–320 (Winter, 1977).

AGRICULTURE
General

"Agriculture," in *Roots*, vol. 2, no. 2 (Winter, 1973–74). 39 p.

Bergquist, J. Gordon. *Summer Boy: Farm Life during the 1920's*. Willmar: The Author, [197-?]. 28 p. Kandiyohi County.

Black, John D. and L. C. Gray. *Land Settlement and Colonization in the Great Lakes States*. (U.S. Dept. of Agriculture Bull. 1295.) Washington: GPO, 1925. 88 p. Northern portions of the states.

Drache, Hiram M. *Beyond the Furrow: Some Keys to Successful Farming in the Twentieth Century*. Danville, Ill.: Interstate Printers & Publishers, 1976. Minn. and Red River Valley, pp. 56–94, 167–206, 281–404.

Duin, Edgar C. "Peter M. Gideon: Pioneer Horticulturist," in *MH*, 44:96–103 (Fall, 1974).

Gilman, Rhoda R. "Interpreting Minnesota's Farm Story," in *MH*, 46:31–33 (Spring, 1978).

Hartman, W. A. and J. D. Black. *Economic Aspects of Land Settlement in the Cut-over Region of the Great Lakes States*. (U.S. Dept. of Agriculture Circular 160.) Washington: GPO, 1931. 86 p.

Lettermann, Edward J. *Farming in early Minnesota as shown by the exhibits in the Agricultural Museum of the Ramsey County Historical Society*. St. Paul: The Society, 1961. 46 p. Rev. ed., *Farming in Early Minnesota*. [St. Paul]: Ramsey County Historical Soc., 1966. 96 p.

Loehr, Rodney C. "The Plowing of America: Early Farming around St. Paul," in *Ramsey County History*, vol. 13, no. 1, pp. 3–12 (Spring/Summer, 1977).

Meyer, Ellen W. E. "Our County's Fruit Basket: Growing and Marketing Apples, Grapes, and Berries around Lake Minnetonka from Pioneer Times to the Present," in *Hennepin County History*, vol. 34, no. 3, pp. 9–19 (Fall, 1975).

State–Federal Crop and Livestock Reporting Service (Minnesota–U.S.). *Minnesota Agricultural Prices, 1958–1970*. St. Paul, 1972. 39 p., and *Minnesota Agricultural Prices, 1969–1975*. St. Paul, 1976. 27 p.

Svoboda, Frank D. *Looking Back: A History of Agriculture in Renville County, Minnesota*. [Olivia?]: Renville County Historical Soc., 1976. 197 p.

Vogeler, Ingolf and Thomas Dockendorff. "Central Minnesota: Relic Tobacco Shed Region," in *Pioneer America: The Journal of Historic American Material Culture*, 10:76–83 (Dec., 1978). Tobacco culture in Stearns and Meeker counties, 1920–70. With bibliog.

Winkelmann, Don. "A Case Study of the Exodus of Labor from Agriculture: Minnesota [1950–60]," in *Journal of Farm Economics*, 48:12–21 (Feb., 1966). With bibliog.

Cattle and Dairying

Meyer, Ellen W. "Dairying around Lake Minnetonka," in *Hennepin County History*, vol. 36, no. 3, pp. 3–14, no. 4, pp. 10–17 (Fall, 1977, Winter, 1977–78).

Todd County Bicentennial Dairy Committee. *The Minutemen of Yesterday, Today and Tomorrow: A Tribute to Todd County's Agricultural Heritage*. N.p., 1976. 97 p.

Wayne, Ralph W. *A Century of Minnesota Dairying and Registered Holsteins, 1876–1976*. N.p.: Minn. Holstein Breeders Assn., [1977]. 209 p.

Education

Pond, George A. and others. *The First Sixty Years of Farm Management Research in Minnesota, 1902–1962*. (Univ. of Minn. Dept. of Agricultural Economics Report 283.) St. Paul, 1965. 63 p.

Thompson, Mark J. *Reminiscences of 90 Years in Minnesota*. N.p.: Privately published, 1973. 30 p. Northeast Experiment Station, Univ. of Minn., Duluth.

Whitaker, James W., ed. "Farming in the Midwest, 1840–1900: A Symposium," in *Agricultural History*, 48:1–220 (Jan., 1974). Includes Joseph C. Fitzharris, "Science for the Farmer: The Development of the

Minnesota Agricultural Experiment Station, 1868–1910," pp. 202–214.

Organizations

Bosch, John H. "Recollections of Rural Revolt: An Interview from the Oral History Collection of the Southwest Minnesota Historical Center," ed. by David L. Nass, in *MH*, 44:304–308 (Winter, 1975). Farmers' Holiday Assn.

Future Farmers of America, Minnesota Association. *25 Years of FFA Activities at the Minnesota State Fair, 1948–1973.* [St. Paul]: FFA Dept., Minn. State Fair, 1973. 32 p.

Zeller, Mary E. *Minnesota State Grange Centennial History.* [Brownsdale]: State Grange, 1972. 82 p.

BUSINESS, INDUSTRY, AND TRADE

General

"Becoming an Industrial State," in *Roots*, vol. 7, no. 1 (Fall, 1978). 31 p.

Burch, Edward P. "Electrical Engineering in Minnesota, 1881 to 1889," in Minn. Federation of Architectural and Engineering Societies, *Bulletin*, vol. 19, no. 7, pp. 5–7 (July, 1934).

Cohen, Henry. *Business and Politics in America from the Age of Jackson to the Civil War: The Career Biography of W. W. Corcoran.* Westport, Conn.: Greenwood Pub. Corp., 1971. "The Great Superior Scheme: Continental Ambitions in Townsites, Railroads, and Politics," pp. 159–201, 331–354.

Fridley, Russell W. "Public Policy and Minnesota's Economy—A Historical View," in *MH*, 44:175–184 (Spring, 1975).

Kreuter, Gretchen. "Empire on the Orinoco: Minnesota Concession in Venezuela," in *MH*, 43:198–212 (Summer, 1973).

Larson, Don W. *Land of the Giants: A History of Minnesota Business.* Minneapolis: Dorn Books, 1979. 176 p.

Lettermann, Edward J. "North St. Paul's 'Manufactories' Come–Back—After 1893 'Bust', " in *Ramsey County History*, vol. 9, no. 1, pp. 17–22 (Spring, 1972).

Mindak, William A. and others. "Economic Effects of the [1962] Minneapolis Newspaper Strike," in *Journalism Quarterly*, 40:213–218 (Spring, 1963).

Minnesota Dept. of Economic Development. *Minnesota Success Stories.* St. Paul, 1980. [17] p. Renal Systems, Mpls.; Jennie–O Foods, Willmar; E. F. Johnson Co., Waseca; Mama Vitale's Frozen Foods, St. Paul.

Northwest Bancorporation. *25 Years of Economic Development: Seven State Northwest Area—Iowa, Minnesota, Montana, Nebraska, North Dakota, South Dakota and Wisconsin.* [Minneapolis], 1954. 68 p.

Supplement to 1953 annual report, covering 1928–53 in statistics.

Scott, Earl P. *The Growth of Minority Business in the Twin Cities Metropolitan Area, 1969–1975.* Minneapolis: Center for Urban and Regional Affairs, Univ. of Minn., 1976. 84 p.

Lumbering

Boorman, George. *Life on a Log Drive.* Gonvick: Richards Pub. Co., Inc., 1980. 19 p. Describes 1937 log drive on Little Fork River.

DeLaittre, Joseph A. *A Story of Early Lumbering in Minnesota.* [Minneapolis]: DeLaittre–Dixon, 1959. 43 p. Reprinted with an additional chapter, 1969.

Hallberg, Jane, ed. *Tales of Local Minnesota Lumberjacks.* Brooklyn Center: Brooklyn Historical Soc., 1978. 12 p.

Hanft, Robert M. *Red River: Paul Bunyan's Own Lumber Company and Its Railroads.* Chico: California State Univ., [1980?]. 304 p. The association of Paul Bunyan stories with the firm's advertising department, with illustrated examples, pp. 209–223.

Hedstrom, Margaret. *Hedstrom Lumber Company: After 60 Years, 1914–1974.* N.p.: Privately published, 1974. 10 p. Near Grand Marais.

Krenz, Duane. "Northern Timber," in *Range History*, vol. 4, no. 2, pp. 1–8 (June, 1979). Virginia area and Virginia and Rainy Lake Co.

"Lumbering in Minnesota," in *Roots*, vol. 4, no. 1 (Fall, 1975). 39 p.

Minnesota Dept. of Natural Resources, Div. of Lands and Forestry. *Forestry in Minnesota.* St. Paul, 1971. 70 p.

Minnesota Timber Producers Assn. *Logging Today Is Different: An Historical Review of the Minnesota Timber Producers Association.* Duluth, 1969. 28 p.

Neils, Paul. *Julius Neils and the J. Neils Lumber Company.* Seattle: Frank McCaffrey, 1971. Minn. activities, pp. 13–41, 48–52.

Rajala, Benhart. *The Saga of Ivar Rajala: Logging in Busticagan [sic] Township, Bigfork River Valley.* Grand Rapids: Ensign Press, 1972. 40 p. Itasca County.

Ryan, J. C. *Early Loggers in Minnesota.* 3 vols. Duluth: Minn. Timber Producers Assn., 1973–80. First published as "Loggers of the Past," in *Timber Producers Association Bulletin*, Oct.–Nov., 1969–Feb.–Mar., 1976. Largely Bemidji, Cloquet, and Duluth areas.

Swanholm, Marx. *Lumbering in the Last of the White-Pine States.* (Minn. Historic Sites Pamphlet Series 17.) St. Paul: MHS, 1978. 36 p. With bibliog.

Vandersluis, Charles, ed. *Mainly Logging: A Compilation.* Minneota: Mineota Clinic, 1974. 372 p. Includes Euclid J. Bourgeois, "Thoughts while Strolling;" John G. Morrison, Jr., "Never a Dull Moment;"

Charles L. Wight, "Reminiscences of a Cruiser." With bibliog.

Wells, Robert W. *"Daylight in the Swamp!"* Garden City, N.Y.: Doubleday, 1978. Minn., pp. 205–240 and *passim.*

Winton, David J. *Ws Back to Back.* N.p.: Privately published, 1971. 165 p. The Winton companies, Wisconsin to the Pacific Coast.

Mining and Quarrying
GENERAL

Alanen, Arnold R. "The Planning of Company Communities in the Lake Superior Mining Region," in Am. Planning Assn., *Journal,* 45:256–278 (July, 1979). With bibliog.

"Mining," in *Roots,* vol. 2, no. 3 (Spring, 1974). 31 p.

Walker, David A. "Lake Vermilion Gold Rush," in *MH,* 44:42–54 (Summer, 1974).

IRON MINING

Boese, Donald L. *John C. Greenway and the Opening of the Western Mesabi.* N.p.: Joint Bovey–Coleraine Bi-Centennial Commission, 1975. 222 p.

Bolf, Peter. "The Pioneering Butlers," in *Range History,* vol. 4, no. 4, pp. 1–10 (Dec., 1979). The Butler brothers' mining activities on the Mesabi Range.

Duncan, Kenneth. *Men of Ore: A Personal History, Given before the St. Louis County Historical Society, November 23, 1965.* N.p.: Tower–Soudan Historical Soc., 1968. 26 p.

Earney, Fillmore C. F. *Researchers' Guide to Iron Ore: An Annotated Bibliography on the Economic Geography of Iron Ore.* Littleton, Colo.: Libraries Unlimited, 1974. Minn., pp. 478–502.

Hendrick, Burton J. *The Life of Andrew Carnegie.* 2 vols. Garden City, N.Y.: Doubleday, 1932. "The Growth of the Carnegie Domain (1893–1900)," 2:1–23. Mesabi Range.

Perry, David E. "Exploratory Diamond Drilling on the Mesabi, 1890 to 1910," in *Range History,* vol. 5, no. 3, pp. 1–10 (Fall, 1980).

Ross, Carl. *The Finn Factor in American Labor, Culture and Society.* New York Mills: Parta Printers, 1977. "Strike [in 1907] on the Mesabi," pp. 106–118.

Walker, David A. *Iron Frontier: The Discovery and Early Development of Minnesota's Three Ranges.* St. Paul: MHS, 1979. 315 p.

QUARRYING

Johnson, Mrs. Carlyle. *History of Jasper Stone Company.* Jasper: Civic Club, 1976. 8 p. Pipestone County.

J. L. Shiely Co. *The J. L. Shiely Company in the Decade of the '80s.* [St. Paul?, 1980?]. [16] p. St. Paul manufacturer of crushed rock.

Manufacturing
MISCELLANEOUS

American Crystal Sugar Co. *50 Years in the Valley: The Story of East Grand Forks, American Crystal's Flagship Plant.* Moorhead, [1974?]. [21]p.

Hudson [H. D.] Manufacturing Co. *The History of the H. D. Hudson Manufacturing Company.* Chicago, [1976]. [16] p. Agricultural equipment; Hastings, Minneapolis, and elsewhere.

Memoirs of a Giant: Green Giant Company's First 75 Years, 1903–1978. N.p.: Privately published, 1978. [40] p.

Meyer, Herbert W. E. *The Early History of the Electric Machinery Mfg. Company.* Rev. ed. N.p.: Privately published, 1973. 10 p. Minneapolis firm.

Minnesota Mining and Manufacturing Co. *Our Story So Far: Notes from the First 75 Years of 3M Company.* St. Paul, 1977. 130 p.

Ott, Virginia and Gloria Swanson. *Man with a Million Ideas: Fred Jones, Genius/Inventor.* Minneapolis: Lerner Pub. Co., 1977. 109 p. Inventor of refrigeration equipment.

Ryder, Franklin J. "Henry Ford's Minneapolis Assembly Plants," in *Hennepin County History,* vol. 32, no. 3, pp. 4–13 (Summer, 1973).

Thomas, Norman F. *Minneapolis–Moline: A History of Its Formation and Operations.* [New York]: Arno Press, 1976. 318 p. With bibliog.

Tyrrell, George. *Potters and Pottery of New Ulm, Minnesota.* [Rochester?]: Privately published, 1978. 92 p. With bibliog.

Viel, Lyndon C. *The Clay Giants: The Stoneware of Red Wing, Goodhue County, Minnesota.* Des Moines, Iowa: Wallace–Homestead Book Co., 1977. 128 p. Mainly a catalog.

Virtue, G. O. "The Co-operative Coopers of Minneapolis," in *Quarterly Journal of Economics,* 19:527–544 (Aug., 1905).

Volkin, David and Henry Bradford. *American Crystal Sugar: Its Rebirth as a Cooperative.* (Farmer Cooperative Service, Dept. of Agriculture FCS Information 98.) Washington: GPO, 1975. 25 p. Red River Valley.

Ziegler, [William H.] Co. *Developing with Minnesota, 1914–1954.* Minneapolis, 1954. 39 p. Heavy machinery manufacture.

FLOUR AND OTHER GRAIN PRODUCTS

Allyn, Karol. *The Peavey Company Flour Mill, Hastings, Minnesota.* N.p.: Privately published, 1975. [8] p.

Dunwiddie, Foster W. "The Six Flouring Mills on Minnehaha Creek," in *MH,* 44:162–174 (Spring, 1975).

Empson, Donald. "John Ayd's Grist Mill—and Reserve Township History," in *Ramsey County History,* vol. 11, no. 2, pp. 3–7 (Fall, 1974).

"Flour Milling," in *Roots*, vol. 3, no. 2 (Winter, 1974). 31 p.

Frame, Robert M., III. *Millers to the World: Minnesota's Nineteenth Century Water Power Flour Mills.* St. Paul: MHS, 1977. 159 p. With bibliog.

_____. "Mills, Machines and Millers: Minnesota Sources for Flour–Milling Research," in *MH*, 46:152–162 (Winter, 1978).

Friedrich, Manfred and Donald Bull. *The Register of United States Breweries, 1876–1976.* Trumbull, Conn.: Privately published, 1976. 2 vols. Arranged by state in vol. 1 and alphabetically in vol. 2.

Huck, Virginia. *Franklin and Harriet: The Crosby Family Story.* Minneapolis: Crosby Co., 1980. 247 p. With bibliog. Early years of a Minneapolis milling company family.

Jacob Schmidt Brewing Co. *Our History.* St. Paul, [1972?]. [7] p.

Kennedy, Gerald S. *Minutes and Moments in the Life of General Mills.* Minneapolis: The Author, 1971. 270 p.

Lundin, Vernard E. *The Hubbard Milling Company, 1878–1978.* Minneapolis: T. S. Denison, 1978. 191 p. Based at Mankato.

Morgan, Dan. *Merchants of Grain.* New York: Viking Press, 1979. 387 p. Minneapolis companies.

One Hundred Years of Brewing . . . Historical Sketches and Views of Ancient and Modern Breweries. Lives and Portraits of Brewers of the Past and Present. Chicago and New York: H. S. Rich, 1903. Reprinted, Newtown, Conn.: Sonja and Will Anderson, 1973. Minn. breweries, pp. 241, 242, 252, 340–347, 431–434, 513–517; malting, 599.

Simms, James Y., Jr. "Impact of Russian Famine, 1891–1892, upon the United States," in *Mid–America*, 60: 171–184 (Oct., 1978). Activities of *Northwestern Miller* and the Farmers' Alliance.

Construction

Associated General Contractors of Minnesota. *50 Years of Service to the Construction Industry: 50th Anniversary, 1919–1969.* Minneapolis, 1969. 96 p.

Ruble, Kenneth D. *The Magic Circle: A Story of the Men and Women Who Made Andersen the Most Respected Name in Windows.* St. Paul: North Central Pub. Co., 1978. 216 p.

Money, Banking, and Insurance

Arnott, Hermon J. *Approaching the Centennial.* Minneapolis: Farmers and Mechanics Savings Bank, 1974. [227] p. With bibliog.

Chucker, Harold. *Banco at Fifty: A History of Northwest Bancorporation, 1929–1979.* Minneapolis: The Company, 1979. 71 p.

First National Bank & Trust Co. of Minneapolis. *75 Years of Service.* N.p., 1939. 27 p.

Fletcher, Abbott L. *History of Minnesota Blue Cross.* N.p.: Privately published, [1970?]. 115 p.

Fridley, Russell W. "A City and a Savings Bank," in *Hennepin County History*, vol. 33, no. 3, pp. 4–22 (Fall, 1974). Farmers and Mechanics Savings Bank, Minneapolis.

Jacobsen, Hazel M. *Northwestern Bank: 1976 Bicentennial History.* Hastings: Northwestern National Bank, 1976. [17] p. Former German American Bank, Hastings, Dakota County.

Karlstad State Bank. *Golden Anniversary, 1925–1975.* Karlstad, 1975. 34 p. Kittson County.

Lund, Doniver A. *Billions for Homes: The TCF Story.* [Minneapolis?]: The Company, 1980. 191 p. Twin City Federal Savings and Loan Assn. of Minneapolis, 1923–79.

_____. *50 Years: A History of First Federal, Minneapolis.* Minneapolis: First Federal Savings and Loan Assn., 1976. 95 p.

Northwestern National Bank of Minneapolis. *100 Years of Service, 1872–1972.* [Minneapolis, 1972]. [16] p.

Rockholt, R[aymond] H. *Minnesota Obsolete Notes and Scrip.* Iola, Wis.: Krause Publications, 1973. 76 p. With bibliog.

Williams, Willis L. *To Commemorate the 80th Birthday of Otto Bremer, by His Associated Banks.* N.p.: Privately published, 1947. [19] p. Reprinted from *Commercial West*, Oct. 25, 1947. American National (of St. Paul) and other banks.

Wholesale and Retail Trade and Service Industries

"Drummers Accommodated: A Nineteenth–Century Salesman in Minnesota," in *MH*, 46:59–65 (Summer, 1978). On Albert D. Onion, based on an article by Margaret K. Onion.

Feltl, Stanley B. "Ice Harvesting on Shady Oak Lake," in *Hennepin County History*, vol. 36, no. 3, pp. 15–19 (Fall, 1977).

Galvin, Kevin. "The Necessities of Life—Available Early on the Frontier," in *Ramsey County History*, vol. 11, no. 2, pp. 8–14 (Fall, 1974). St. Paul.

Gray, James. *Our First Century: The Story of General Trading Company, Serving Transportation's Needs Since the Days of the Oxcart.* St. Paul: The Company, 1955. [98] p. Text on even–numbered pages only.

Hanes, John K. *The Organization of Wholesale Fruit and Vegetable Markets in Minneapolis–St. Paul and Duluth–Superior.* (U.S. Dept. of Agriculture Marketing Research Report 647.) Washington, 1964. 42 p. With bibliog.

Hendrickson, Robert. *The Grand Emporiums: The Illustrated History of America's Great Department*

Stores. New York: Stein and Day, 1979. 488 p. Includes Dayton's, Gamble–Skogmo, and Duluth Glass Block.

Hess, Jeffrey A. *Alexander Harkin, Dealer in Dry Goods and Groceries.* (Minn. Historic Sites Pamphlet Series 14.) St. Paul: MHS, 1977. 24 p.

Kahler Corporation. *60 Years of Caring: The Kahler Corporation, 1917–1977.* [Rochester?], 1977. 27 p. Hotels.

Lampert Lumber Co. *They Used to Call Them Lumberyards: The Story of the Lampert Lumber Company.* St. Paul, [1976]. 35 p.

Mahoney, Tom and Leonard Sloane. *The Great Merchants: America's Foremost Retail Institutions and the People Who Made Them Great.* 3rd ed. New York: Harper, 1974. "Dayton's and Hudson's: The Giants of Minneapolis and Detroit," pp. 215–228, 391.

Martin, Albro. "James J. Hill and the First Energy Revolution: A Study in Entrepreneurship, 1865–1878," in *Business History Review,* 50:179–197 (Summer, 1976). Coal trade in St. Paul.

Nassig, George W. "Ice Harvesting, Storage and Distribution," in *Hennepin County History,* vol. 37, no. 2, pp. 14–22 (Summer, 1978).

National Society of the Colonial Dames of America. *Three Centuries of Custom Houses.* N.p., 1972. Lydia C. Schrader, "Minnesota," pp. 281–287, 354. With bibliog.

Otis, Arthur R. *The Challenge of Sissebakwet.* N.p.: Privately published, 1976. Resort ownership in Itasca County, pp. 91–129.

[Plymouth Clothing House]. *A Brief Record of the History of the Plymouth and of Early Minneapolis, 1882–1922.* Minneapolis, 1922. [39] p.

Rosén, Axel. "Buying Lots on the Installment Plan," in *The Bridge* (Karlstad, Swed.), 8:8–13 (1976). Johnson Brothers, Minneapolis.

Rudensky, Morris ("Red") and Don Riley. *The Gonif . . . Red Rudensky.* Blue Earth: Piper Co., 1970. 215 p. St. Paul business career with Brown and Bigelow and 3M, 1944–70, pp. 147–181.

Staples, Loring M. *The West Hotel Story, 1884–1940: Memories of Past Splendor.* Minneapolis: Carlson Printing Co., 1979. 136 p.

Thorstenson, Ruth Z. "The West Hotel," in *Hennepin County History,* vol. 37, no. 3, pp. 3–9, no. 4, pp. 13–21 (Fall, 1978, Winter, 1978–79); vol. 38, no. 1, pp. 3–11 (Spring, 1979). Minneapolis.

CO-OPERATIVE MOVEMENT
Farmers' Co-operatives

Argyle Cooperative Warehouse Association. *75th Anniversary, Argyle Cooperative Warehouse Association, 1905–1980.* Stephen: Messenger Print, [1980]. 24 p. Marshall County.

Farmers Union Marketing & Processing Association. *Milestones in Cooperation: Farmers Union Marketing and Processing Association, 1929–1979.* Redwood Falls, 1979. 25 p.

Lamphere, Lyle. *They Charted the Course: The History of Central Livestock Association, Inc.* N.p.: The Association, 1971. [11] p.

Rickertsen, Leo N. *To Gather Together: CENEX, The First Fifty Years.* Minneapolis: Cooperative Printing Assn., 1980. 272 p.

Ruble, Kenneth D. *Land O' Lakes: Farmers Make It Happen: A Sequel to "Men to Remember."* N.p.: Privately published, 1973. 205 p.

Consumers' Co-operatives

Midland Cooperatives. *Fifty Years of Service.* [Minneapolis], 1976. 48 p.

Nurmi, Maiju, ed. *10th Anniversary Album: A History of the Northern States Women's Co-operative Guild.* Superior, Wis.: The Guild, 1939. Minn. guilds, pp. [20–37, 46].

O'Neil, Cy. "Origins and Legacies: The History of a Co-operative Movement," in *Scoop* (Minneapolis), no. 26, pp. 1–48 (Nov., 1977). Central Co-operative Wholesale in Minn., Mich., and Wis.

COMMUNICATIONS
Radio, Television, and Telephone

Beck, George A. *A Brief History and Purposes of Educational Television and of the Duluth–Superior Area Educational Television Corporation, Operator of WDSE–TV Channel 8.* N.p.: WDSE–TV, 1979. 36 p.

Beck, Joe. "Pioneering in Television in the Twin Cities," in *MH,* 46:274–285 (Fall, 1979).

Rippey, James C. *Goodbye, Central; Hello, World: A Centennial History of Northwestern Bell.* Omaha: Northwestern Bell, 1975. 344 p. Minn., *passim.*

WCCO–TV (Television Station), Minneapolis. *Since 1949.* [Minneapolis?, 1979?]. [20] p.

Williams, Bob and Chuck Hartley. *Good Neighbor to the Northwest, 1924–1974.* [Minneapolis?]: WCCO, 1974. 120 p. WCCO Radio.

Books, Newspapers, and Journalists

Endres, Kathleen. "Jane Grey Swisshelm: 19th Century Journalist and Feminist," in *Journalism History,* 4:128–132 (1975–76).

Friendly, Fred W. "Censorship and Journalists' Privilege: The Case of Near *versus* Minnesota—a Half Century Later," in *MH,* 46:147–151 (Winter, 1978).

McCarthy, Abigail. "Jane Grey Swisshelm: Marriage and Slavery," in Barbara Stuhler and Gretchen Kreuter, eds., *Women of Minnesota: Selected Biographical Essays*. St. Paul: MHS, 1977, pp. 34–54.

Marzolf, Marion T. *The Danish–Language Press in America*. (Scandinavians in America Series.) New York: Arno Press, 1979. 276 p. Christian Rasmussen, pp. 83–90; Minn., *passim*.

Rippley, La Vern J. "Notes About the German Press in the Minnesota River Valley," in Soc. for the History of the Germans in Maryland, *The Report: A Journal of German–American History*, 35:37–45 (1972). Reprinted, Don H. Tolzmann, ed. *German–American Literature*. Metuchen, N.J.: Scarecrow Press, 1977, pp. 70–82; and in *Currents* (Shakopee), 1:5–12 (Spring, 1979).

Tolzmann, Don H. "Minnesota's German–American Book Trade: 1850–1935," in *American Book Collector*, 24:20–22 (July–Aug., 1974).

Treckel, Paula A. "Jane Grey Swisshelm and Feminism in Early Minnesota," in *Midwest Review*, 2nd series, 2:1–17 (Spring, 1980).

U.S. Mail and Post Offices

Patera, Alan H. and John S. Gallagher. *The Post Offices of Minnesota*. Burtonsville, Md.: The Depot, 1978. 280 p. Arranged alphabetically by county, with names, dates of operation, and first postmasters.

Tunheim, John R. "Country Post Offices [in New Folden Township, Marshall County]," in *Red River Valley Historian*, Winter, 1975–76, pp. 32–38, 40–42, 44.

TRANSPORTATION

Water Transportation

GENERAL

Merritt, Raymond H. *Creativity, Conflict & Controversy: A History of the St. Paul District, U.S. Army Corps of Engineers*. Washington: GPO, 1979. 461 p.

"Minnesota's Rivers," in *Roots*, vol. 6, no. 3 (Spring, 1978). 31 p.

Ryder, Franklin J. *A Century of Service: The Centennial Story of the St. Paul District, Army Corps of Engineers*. 3rd ed. St. Paul: The District, 1972. 32 p. First published in 1966.

U.S. Army Corps of Engineers, Mississippi River Commission. *Annual Highest and Lowest Stages of the Mississippi River and Its Outlets and Tributaries to 1960*. Vicksburg, Miss.: U.S. Army Engineer District, 1961. Aitkin, St. Paul, Hastings, and Winona, pp. 1–8.

NAVIGATION AND IMPROVEMENT ON THE MISSISSIPPI RIVER

Gregory, Winifred. "Improvement of the Upper Mississippi River: A Bibliography," in Affiliated Engineering Societies of Minn., *Bulletin*, 3:167–175 (Sept., 1918).

Nichols, George C. *Recollections of a Pioneer Steamboat Pilot, Contributing to the Early History of the Mississippi River*. La Crosse, Wis.: Tucker & Co., 1883. 40 p.

Niemeyer, Robert H. "Streckfus Steamers," in *Steamboat Bill* (Staten Island, N.Y.), 130:93–97 (Summer, 1974).

NAVIGATION ON LAKE SUPERIOR

Barry, James P. *Ships of the Great Lakes: 300 Years of Navigation*. Berkeley, Calif.: Howell–North Books, 1973. 256 p. Minn., *passim*.

Fletcher, Daniel O. "The Decline of the Great Lakes Package–Freight Carriers," in *Business History Review*, 36:387–407 (Winter, 1962).

Hall, Stephen P. *Split Rock: Epoch of a Lighthouse*. (Minn. Historic Sites Pamphlet Series 15.) St. Paul: MHS, 1978. 23 p.

LesStrang, Jacques. *Lake Carriers: The Saga of the Great Lakes Fleet—North America's Fresh Water Merchant Marine*. Seattle: Superior Pub. Co., 1977. 192 p.

———. *Seaway: The Untold Story of North America's Fourth Seacoast*. Seattle: Salisbury Press, 1976. 214 p.

Lydecker, Ryck. *Pigboat—The Story of the Whalebacks*. Duluth: Sweetwater Press, 1973. 35 p.

Sandvik, Glenn. *A Superior Beacon: A Brief History of Split Rock Lighthouse*. N.p.: Privately published, 1972. 13 p. Another version published as "A Brief History of the Split Rock Lighthouse," in *Inland Seas*, 28:206–208, 214, 217–222 (Fall, 1972).

Stonehouse, Frederick. *The Great Wrecks of the Great Lake: A Directory of the Shipwrecks of Lake Superior*. Marquette, Mich.: Harboridge Press, 1973. 130 p. With bibliog.

Van der Linden, Peter J., ed. *Great Lakes Ships We Remember*. Cleveland, Ohio: Freshwater Press, 1979. 413 p. Illustrated.

Wolff, Julius F., Jr. *The Shipwrecks of Lake Superior*. Duluth: Lake Superior Marine Museum Assn., 1979. 180 p.

———. "They Sailed Away on Lake Superior," in *Inland Seas*, 29:262–274, 276, 283–285 (Winter, 1973). Addenda, 30:47 (Spring, 1974). Ships that disappeared.

NAVIGATION ON THE RED RIVER

Burdick, Usher L., ed. *Life on the Red River of the North, 1857 to 1887: Being the History of Navigation on the Red River of the North, by Fred A. Bill, and*

Life on the River Towns of Fargo and Moorhead, by
J. W. *Riggs.* Baltimore: Wirth Brothers, 1947. 122 p.
Contains expanded versions of Bill's articles published
in *North Dakota Historical Quarterly,* 2:100–119,
201–216 (Jan., Apr., 1928), plus interviews with Riggs
and James W. Hogges.

Roads and Bridges

Clark, George L. *History of Rice County Roads and
Highway Department under Jurisdiction of the Rice
County Board between 1855 & 1974.* [Faribault?]:
Privately published, 1975. 26 p.

Jacobsen, Hazel M. *The Spiral Bridge of Hastings: Its
Beginning and End.* Hastings: Bicentennial Commission, 1976. 34 p.

Kelly, Ardath B. *Pioneer Roadbuilder: An Historical
Biography.* [Red Lake?]: Privately published, 1978.
177 p. Roy K. Bliler, highway engineer in northern
Minn.

Reese, Herbert R., Sr. *Seventy Years Down the Road.*
Hawley: Herald, 1973. 130 p. Road building and
trucking in northern Minn.

Sanford, Sidney. *The Wheat Trail.* [Verndale: Historical
Soc., 1976]. 4 p., map. A wagon road from the Hubbard County line south to wheat market at Verndale.

Singley, Grover. *Tracing Minnesota's Old Government
Roads.* (Minn. Historic Sites Pamphlet Series 10.)
St. Paul: MHS, 1974. 52 p.

Trails

Bearss, Edwin C. and Bruce M. White. "George Brack-
ett's Wagon Road: Minnesota Enterprise on a New
Frontier," in *MH,* 45:42–57 (Summer, 1976).

Gilman, Carolyn. "Perceptions of the Prairie: Cultural
Contrasts on the Red River Trails," in *MH,* 46:112–
122 (Fall, 1978).

Gilman, Rhoda R. and others. *The Red River Trails:
Oxcart Routes between St. Paul and the Selkirk Settlement, 1820–1870.* St. Paul: MHS, 1979. 105 p.

Reddemann, Ahle. *The Henderson to Fort Ridgely
Trail.* [Henderson]: Sibley County Historical Soc.,
1976. 65 p.

Autos, Buses, and Streetcars

Bailey, Anne S. *. . . With Safety for All . . . Minnesota Safety Council: A Fifty-Year History.* St. Paul:
The Council, 1978. 235 p.

Lowry, Goodrich. *Streetcar Man: Tom Lowry and the
Twin City Rapid Transit Company.* Minneapolis:
Lerner, 1979. 177 p.

Olson, Russell L. *The Electric Railways of Minnesota.*
Hopkins: Minn. Transportation Museum, 1976. 560 p.
Mainly street railways.

Quist, Helmer. *1920 Tourists: The Quists.* Lafayette:
Ledger Printing Co., [1969?]. 20 p. An auto tour from

St. James, Minn., to Calif., Ore., Wash., Ida., Mont.,
and N.D.

Weckman, Violet M. "J. Victor Maryland, Pioneer Bus-
man," in *Range History,* vol. 5, no. 2, pp. 1–6 (Summer, 1980).

Railroads
GENERAL

Dorin, Patrick C. *The Lake Superior Iron Ore Railroads.*
Seattle: Superior Pub. Co., 1969. 144 p. Includes Cuyuna Range railroads.

Francaviglia, Richard V. "Some Comments on the Historic and Geographic Importance of Railroads in Minnesota," in *MH,* 43:58–62 (Summer, 1972); and letter
to author by Mrs. John S. Ruenitz, in *MH,* 43:119 (Fall,
1972).

Gilbert, Heather. *The Life of Lord Mount Stephen.*
2 vols. [Aberdeen, Scot.]: Aberdeen Univ. Press,
1965–77. Canadian Pacific–Great Northern–Northern
Pacific relations, *passim,* especially in vol. 2, *The End
of the Road.*

Grant, H. Roger. "Small–Town Railroad Stations on the
Upper Plains: A Pictorial Essay," in *Midwest Review,*
1:35–42 (Spring, 1979). Railroad depots along the
Minneapolis and St. Louis Railroad line between Mor-
ton and Watertown, S.D., and between New Ulm and
Storm Lake, Iowa. Illustrated.

———— and Charles W. Bohi. *The Country Railroad
Station in America.* Boulder, Colo.: Pruett Pub. Co.,
1978. 183 p. Architecture. Minn., *passim.*

Post, Robert C. "Manuscript Sources for Railroad History," in *Railroad History,* no. 137, pp. 38–63 (Autumn, 1977).

"Railroads in Minnesota," in *Roots,* vol. 4, no. 2 (Winter,
1975–76). 31 p.

Saunders, Richard. *The Railroad Mergers and the Coming of Conrail.* Westport, Conn.: Greenwood Press,
1978. Minn. involvement, pp. 156–165, 225–245.

Smith, Fannie B. *Reminiscences of George M. Smith,
and His Connection with the Railroads of the Northwest.* N.p.: Privately published, 1935. [16] p.

White, Bruce M. "Working for the Railroad: Life in the
General Offices of the Great Northern and Northern
Pacific, 1915–21," in *MH,* 46:24–30 (Spring, 1978).

Working on the Railroad. Waseca: County Historical
Soc., 1980. 16 p. Waseca County.

CHICAGO, MILWAUKEE,
ST. PAUL AND PACIFIC

Dorin, Patrick C. *The Milwaukee Road East: America's
Resourceful Railroad.* Seattle: Superior Pub. Co.,
1978. 175 p.

Greenberg, Dolores. "A Study of Capital Alliances: The
St. Paul & Pacific," in *Canadian Historical Review,*
57:25–39 (Mar., 1976).

Mitchell, F. Stewart. "The Chicago, Milwaukee & St. Paul Railway and James J. Hill in Dakota Territory, 1879–1885," in *North Dakota History*, 47:11–19 (Fall, 1980).

Schmidt, William H., Jr. "The Singular Milwaukee—A Profile," in *Railroad History*, no. 136, pp. 5–129 (Spring, 1977).

JAMES J. HILL AND THE GREAT NORTHERN

Best, Gary D. "James J. Hill's 'Lost Opportunity on the Pacific'," in *Pacific Northwest Quarterly*, 64:8–11 (Jan., 1973). Great Northern Steamship Line.

Josephson, Matthew. *The Robber Barons: The Great American Capitalists, 1861–1901*. New York: Harcourt, Brace and Co., 1934. James J. Hill, pp. 231–252, 432–453.

Martin, Albro. *James J. Hill and the Opening of the Northwest*. New York: Oxford Univ. Press, 1976. 676 p.

———. "James J. Hill: Enterpreneur [sic] in the Classic Mold," in *Journal of the West*, 17:62–74 (Oct., 1978).

Martin, Charles F. *Locomotives of the Empire Builder: A Railbuff's Primer of Steam on the Great Northern Railway*. Chicago: Normandie House, 1972. [84] p. With bibliog. Illustrated.

Middleton, Kenneth R. and Norman C. Keyes, Jr. "The Great Northern Railway Company: Predecessors and Fully–Controlled Subsidiaries," and "The Great Northern Railway Company: All Time Locomotive Roster, 1861–1970," in *Railroad History*, no. 143, pp. 8–19, 20–162 (Autumn, 1980).

Mountfield, David. *The Railway Barons*. New York: Norton, 1979. "Last of the Empire Builders," pp. 159–217, on James J. Hill.

Sobel, Robert. *The Entrepreneurs: Explorations within the American Business Tradition*. New York: Weybright and Talley, 1974. "James J. Hill: The Business of Empire," pp. 110–147.

Wood, Charles R. and Dorothy M. Wood. *The Great Northern Railway: A Pictorial Study*. Edmonds, Wash.: Pacific Fast Mail, 1979. 560 p. With bibliog.

NORTHERN PACIFIC

Cotroneo, Ross R. "The Great Northern Pacific Plan of 1927," in *Pacific Northwest Quarterly*, 54:104–112 (July, 1963).

Leverty, Maureen J., comp. *Guide to Records of the Northern Pacific Branch Lines, Subsidiaries, and Related Companies in the Minnesota Historical Society*. St. Paul: MHS, 1977. 13 p.

Renz, Louis T. *The History of the Northern Pacific Railroad*. Fairfield, Wash.: Galleon Press, 1980. 288 p.

Schwietz, William T. *The Gladstone Shops of the St. Paul and Duluth R.R.* St. Paul: [The author?], 1977. 18 p.

Smalley, Eugene V. *History of the Northern Pacific Railroad*. New York: Putnam, 1883. 437 p. Reprinted, New York: Arno Press, 1975.

Ward, James A. *That Man Haupt: A Biography of Herman Haupt*. Baton Rouge: Louisiana State Univ. Press, 1973. "Main Street of the Northwest," pp. 217–233.

OTHER RAILROAD COMPANIES

Dorin, Patrick C. *Everywhere West: The Burlington Route*. Seattle: Superior Pub. Co., 1976. 171 p.

———. *The Soo Line*. Seattle: Superior Pub. Co., 1979. 192 p.

Gjevre, John A. *Saga of the Soo, West from Shoreham: An Illustrated History of the Soo Line Railroad Company and Its Predecessors in Minnesota, the Dakotas and Montana*. La Crosse, Wis.: Privately published, 1973. 111 p. With bibliog.

Jacobsen, Hazel M. *Hastings: From River to Rails on the H & D*. [Hastings?]: The Author, 1975. 12 p. An informal account of the Hastings and Dakota Railroad, chartered in 1856 and constructed in 1868.

"Our Story of Steam," in *Missabe Iron Ranger* (Duluth), Apr., 1961, pp. 1–50. Duluth, Missabe, and Iron Range Railroad.

Aviation

Allard, Noel E. *Speed: The Biography of Charles W. Holman*. Chaska: Privately published, 1976. 86 p.

Carley, Kenneth. "Lindbergh in Song," in *MH*, 45:192–194 (Spring, 1977). Charles A. Lindbergh, Jr.

Gill, Brendan. *Lindbergh Alone*. New York: Harcourt Brace Jovanovich, 1977. 216 p.

Lindbergh, Charles A., Jr. *Autobiography of Values*. New York: Harcourt Brace Jovanovich, 1978. 423 p. With bibliog. of Lindbergh's writings.

———. "Some Remarks at Dedication of Lindbergh State Park Interpretive Center," in *MH*, 43:275 (Fall, 1973).

Mills, Stephen E. *A Pictorial History of Northwest Airlines*. New York: Bonanza Books, 1980. 192 p. With bibliog. First published as *More Than Meets the Sky*. Seattle: Superior Pub. Co., 1972.

Serling, Robert J. *Ceiling Unlimited: The Story of North Central Airlines*. Marceline, Mo.: Walsworth Pub. Co., 1973. 245 p.

Ward, John W. "[Charles A.] Lindbergh and the Meaning of American Society," in *MH*, 45:288–291 (Fall, 1977).

PUBLIC UTILITIES

Cooperative Light and Power Association of Lake County. *Your Cooperative Light & Power Association of Lake County, Two Harbors, Minnesota, 1936–1961.* [Two Harbors, 1961]. [34] p.

Joesting, Ted W. *The Utilities of Owatonna: A Compendium, 1854–1970.* Owatonna: Photo News, 1972. 476 p.

Jones, Stiles P. "The Minneapolis Gas Settlement: A Typical Struggle for a City's Rights," in Clyde L. King, ed., *The Regulation of Municipal Utilities.* New York: Appleton, 1912, pp. 56–72.

Meyer, Herbert W. *A History of the Divisions of the Northern States Power Company.* Minneapolis: The Company, 1957. 141 p.

Pine, Carol. *NSP, Northern States People: The Past 70 Years.* Minneapolis: The Company, 1979. 144 p.

Index

Users of this index are warned that more than one entry on a given subject may appear on a page and that the entire page cited should be checked.